Formal Methods in Standards

A Report from the BCS Working Group

C.L.N. Ruggles (Ed.)

Formal Methods in Standards

A Report from the BCS Working Group

Principal Contributors:

Derek Andrews
David Blyth
Cornelia Boldyreff
David Duce
Patrick Hall

Robert Neely
Clive Ruggles
Nik Tetteh-Lartey
Rick Thomas
Ann Wrightson

Springer-Verlag
London Berlin Heidelberg New York
Paris Tokyo Hong Kong

C.L.N. Ruggles
Department of Computing Studies, University of Leicester,
University Road, Leicester LE1 7RH, UK

ISBN-13: 978-3-540-19577-1   e-ISBN-13: 978-1-4471-3419-0
DOI: 10.1007/978-1-4471-3419-0

British Library Cataloguing in Publication Data
Formal methods in standards: a report from the BCS Working Group.
  1. Computer systems, Standards
  I. Ruggles, Clive, *1952*– II. Andrews, Derek III. BCS Working Group
004.0218
ISBN-13: 978-3-540-19577-1

Library of Congress Cataloging-in-Publication Data
Formal methods in standards:a report from the BCS Working Group/
C.L.N. Ruggles, editor; principal contributors, Derek Andrews . . . [et. al.].
  p. cm.
  Includes bibliographical references and index.
  ISBN-13: 978-3-540-19577-1
1. Electronic data processing–Standards–Great Britain
I. Ruggles, C. L. N. (Clive L. N.) II. Andrews, Derek. III. British Computer
Society. Formal Methods in Standards Working Group.
QA76.9.S8F67 1990   90-35889
004′.0218–dc20   CIP

2128/3916–543210 Printed on acid-free paper

Contents

Overview

This document attempts to identify general issues that relate to the introduction of formal methods into the development and expression of standards, and to offer general guidelines on the use of formal methods for those working in different standards areas. It is produced by the Formal Methods in Standards Working Group of the British Computer Society (BCS). A brief description of the Group and summary of its terms of reference are given in Section 1.

Section 2 identifies the primary concepts, and describes the aims and principles, of standardisation. This is followed in Section 3 by an outline survey covering the definition and usage of a selection of formal and semi-formal methods and associated support tools.

Case studies of practice to date are then presented in four distinct application areas: programming languages (Section 4.2), document structure (Section 4.3), graphics (Section 4.4) and open systems interconnection (Section 4.5).

Section 5 addresses the general question of how formal methods can improve the quality of standards, drawing upon an assessment of practice to date, and offers some general guidelines for the application of formal methods in standards.

The bibliography is in two parts: a bibliography of standards and a general bibliography. References to standards are given in round brackets thus: (ISO 8879). Where ISO standards are also British standards an indication of the BSI number is given in the bibliography entry. General references are given in square brackets thus: [Chu36].

There are two appendices: a list of common acronyms (Appendix *A*) and a glossary of formal methods terminology (Appendix *B*). All acronyms used without explanation in the main text are listed in Appendix *A*. Where a term defined in the glossary is first used in the main text, it is italicised, thus indicating that a glossary definition exists.

Acknowledgements

The Working Group is grateful to David Barker and Bob King of NCC Ltd. for providing written contributions to the document and to Wolfgang Appelt of GMD and to Angela Mison of NCC Ltd. who read and commented upon sections of the manuscript. We are also grateful to Jackie Macklin of the University of Leicester for her assistance in keying in parts of the manuscript.

The glossary (Appendix *B*) is included by kind permission of ICL for whom it was originally prepared by one of the contributors (David Blyth) as part of a consulting document. The present edition has been substantially edited and revised from the original.

1.
The Formal Methods in Standards Working Group

The formation of the Formal Methods in Standards Working Group arose from a meeting, held at BCS headquarters, of BCS members involved in standards work. The meeting expressed concern at the lack of informed opinion on the use of formal methods in standards specification, production and verification. It was suggested by Ann Wrightson that a Working Group be set up to tackle the problem. The group was duly formed, initially under the chairmanship of Patrick Hall. He handed over after the first few meetings to Clive Ruggles, the current chairman.

1.1 Terms of reference

The primary objective of the group is to promote the practical application of formal methods in improving the quality of standards used in computer systems and software.

The secondary (enabling) objectives of the group are as follows:

- to identify where the use of formal methods will improve the quality of standards in fitness for purpose, implementability and usability;

- to determine the current situation in respect of formal methods and their practical application in the areas identified;

- to advise BCS members actively involved in standards of the findings of the above and to publish guidelines and recommendations regarding the application and use of formal methods;

- to identify significant areas where further effort is required in the development, application and promotion of formal methods;

- to identify and subsequently liaise with other bodies who are currently active, or can contribute towards, the Group's objectives in order that BCS views may be represented to these bodies;

- to propose a programme of work in the application of formal methods as is considered to be beneficial in meeting the objectives; and

- to devise and undertake an educative programme, through publications, seminars and workshops, which will promote the effective use of formal methods, by BCS members, in improving the quality of standards.

The publication of this report represents a first step by the Group towards the fulfilment of some of these objectives.

1.2 Constitution

The Working Group reports to the BCS Standards Co-ordinator, David Iggulden, who in turn reports to the Technical Board. Staff support is from the Technical Division at BCS Headquarters, which was headed until 1989 by Tony Sale, the technical co-ordinator. Joan Worker and Ellen Thompson have acted as secretaries to the Working Group.

1.3 Modus Operandi

One of the strengths of the group is the breadth of the fields of interest of its members, where general reactions to the use, or attempted use, of formal techniques in standards development are often very different.

The group has attempted to build upon this breadth of experience in order to identify general issues which relate to the introduction of formal techniques into the development and expression of standards, and to offer general guidelines for those working to introduce formal techniques in different standards areas. Its concern is not simply to impart specialist knowledge of particular formal methods.

During the early stages of the Group's work two formative workshops were held (in April and October 1988) at which the principal speakers were Derek Andrews, David Blyth, David Duce, Alan Garnham, Patrick Hall, Darrel Ince, Nik Tetteh-Lartey, and Ken Turner. The discussions at these sessions have helped to give rise to this document. This document represents the first major deliverable of the group.

From now onwards the work of the group will concentrate more on education in the form of seminars and courses. The first event will be a workshop primarily aimed at standards makers (rather than users): participation will be restricted to those—BCS members and others—involved in standards bodies, together with members of specialist groups involved in areas of potential use of formal standards. Subsequent events will be aimed more widely at standards users.

1.4 Membership

At present the group comprises approximately twenty members, from academia and industry, actively involved in the application of formal methods in the development and review of standards. Their interests span areas such as communication protocols, the specification of programming languages, graphics standardisation, and document structure.

The membership of the group is as follows:

Chairman	Clive Ruggles	Leicester University
Vice chairman	David Blyth	Incord Ltd.
Technical co-ordinator	Tony Sale	British Computer Society
Members	Derek Andrews	Leicester University
	Cornelia Boldyreff	Brunel University
	David Duce	Rutherford Appleton Labs.
	Patrick Hall	Brunel University
	David Iggulden	ANSA Project
	John Kwok	NHS IT Unit
	Brian Meek	King's College London
	Robert Neely	CITI
	Mike Newton	Open University
	Bill Olle	Independent Consultant
	Graham Parkin	NPL
	Ben Potter	STC
	David Roberts	Neville Clark & Associates
	Tony Rush	Hewlett Packard
	Mike Sykes	ICI
	Nik Tetteh-Lartey	National Computing Centre
	Rick Thomas	Leicester University
	Ann Wrightson	Press Computer Systems Ltd.
Invited contributors	Darrel Ince	Open University
	Alastair Tocher	STL
	Ken Turner	Stirling University
Workshop contributors	Alan Garnham	Sussex University

2.
Standards: the Background

2.1 What is a Standard?

This section identifies the primary concepts, and describes the aims and principles, of standardisation, following [ISO80] and the BSI 'Standard for standards' (BS 0).

2.1.1 Concepts

The objects of standardisation are products, services, processes and practices; and the end of standardisation is agreed standards. The achievement of this end is through the activity of standardisation.

The following definitions are taken from [ISO80]:

- *Standard*. A technical specification or other document available to the public, drawn up with the co-operation and consensus or general approval of all interests affected by it, based on the consolidated results of science, technology and experience, aimed at the promotion of optimum community benefits and approved by a body recognised on the national, regional or international level.

- *Standardisation*. An activity giving solutions for repetitive application, to problems essentially in the spheres of science, technology and economics, aimed at the achievement of the optimum degree of order in a given context. Generally, the activity consists of the processes of formulating, issuing and implementing standards.

- *National standards body*. A nationally recognised body whose principal function at the national level, by virtue of its statutes or the law of the country, is the preparation and/or publication of national standards and/or approval of standards prepared by other bodies. This body is eligible to be the national member of the corresponding international and regional standards organisations.

2.1.2 Why Standardise?

Standardisation promotes consistent quality and economic production. The motivation for standards can be summarised as follows:

- the need for a basis for communication and interchangeability;

- the need for economic production and interworking of standardised products and services;

- the need for adequate and consistent quality and fitness for purpose of goods and services; and

- the promotion of trade through international agreement.

2.1.3   Principles of Standardisation

The principles of standardisation are consensus, usability, feasibility and har-monisation. It must be agreed that the standard is wanted. Its intended applic-ation should be clearly understood at the start and borne in mind throughout its preparation. The decision to standardise must be based on the user com-munity's agreed needs but must not inhibit technical innovation. The process of standardisation should embrace existing standards in order to achieve har-monisation.

2.1.4   Problems

A report on standards in computing, produced as long ago as 1977 by the National Computing Centre (NCC) for the Department of Trade and Industry, noted that developments in computing had reached a point such that the scope of its applications urgently required a whole framework of standards [NCC77]. The report also stated that in the absence of such standards the proliferation in computing and telecommunications would result in progressively larger prob-lems of interconnection between various systems which would counteract the advantages that the new technology heralded and promised.

Thus it was noted, even in 1977, that standards development was falling behind the pioneering developments in the computing industry and technology. Standards have generally failed to keep pace with the industry ever since. This has resulted in turn in technological advances being held back, with an increas-ing proportion of expenditure and effort being wasted on tackling and circum-venting incompatibility problems. Historical factors, due in part to the late arrival of standards, have been identified as a major contribution to the cur-rent, still chaotic, state of affairs. Factors such as the lack of standards pro-motion and the neglect of training of professionals in the subject have also played a role. A further critical factor, directly resulting from the others, is the very poor level of observance of standards.

The production of standards in computing can be said to be analogous to a quotation attributed to Dr Johnson: '... it is like a dog walking on two legs; it is not done well, but you are amazed to see it done at all'. Faced with the prob-lems of producing standards for such a complex and dynamic technology, it is an achievement in itself that the standards organisations have produced so many standards which affect the international computing community (exclud-ing those SI-Unit standards for hardware—such as nuts, bolts, chair and desk heights—which also affect the general public). It is also no surprise that in the information technology arena the organisations concerned with the standardisation process have not always achieved the precision or timeliness that was originally expected of them in the task of setting standards.

2.2 The Standards-making Structure

2.2.1 The Protagonists

2.2.1.1 Overview

There are many organisations at all levels which are concerned with the production of standards. **ISO** (the **International Organisation for Standardisation**) is the main one; the others include the following.

- **IEC** (the **International Electro-Technical Commission**) is concerned with the electrical safety of computers and with telecommunications standards. In the IT arena the IEC and ISO have formed a Joint Committee to oversee a co-ordinated programme of work on standards development.

- **CCITT** (the **International Telegraph and Telephone Consultative Committee**) is concerned with telecommunications technology standards. Recent agreements and co-operation between ISO and CCITT are presently being used to progress joint projects. Thus, while the CCITT still publishes independently its series of 'Recommendations' in four-yearly cycles, where there is collaboration with IEC and ISO the recommendations are fully aligned.

- **ECMA** (the **European Computer Manufacturers' Association**) is concerned with early agreement by manufacturers. ECMA contributes heavily to ISO and CCITT work.

- **CEN/CENELEC** (the **European Committee for Standardisation** and the **European Committee for Electro-Technical Standardisation**) and **CEPT** (the **European Conference of Postal and Telecommunications Administration**) are bodies which ratify pan-European and functional standards.

- **EWOS** (the **European Workshop on Open Systems**) is a forum set up to create standardised profiles with reference to open systems. Similar bodies exist, for example, in the USA and Japan; all these bodies submit profiles to the ISO/IEC Joint Committee for endorsement as ISPs (International Standard Profiles).

These organisations, in addition to others, have national counterparts in most countries of the industrial world.

- **ANSI** (the **American National Standards Institute**) is a co-ordinating body for standardisation in the USA. It publishes and approves standards from other bodies such as the **IEEE (Institute of Electrical and Electronic Engineers)**.

Apart from ANSI, bodies such as the following perform formative work and approval.

- **AFNOR** (the **French Association for Normalization**).

- **BSI** (the **British Standards Institution**).

- **CSA** (the **Canadian Standards Association**).

- **DIN** (the **German Institute for Normalization**).

- **JISC** (the **Japanese Industrial Standards Committee**).

The activities of these bodies are organised slightly differently in each country.

At present this proliferation of organisations is not considered excessive but rather reflects the genuine complexity and wide scope of information processing technology. It is usual, except between national and international equivalents, to find that there is little commonality in work programmes within organisations. Duplication between equivalent bodies in different countries is, of course, an unavoidable aspect of the standardisation process. Most duplication that arises is productive duplication, with different viewpoints being brought to bear on the same problem. In general the greatest problem in standards is that most standardisation projects lack any powerful driving force. This is a direct result of the standardisation effort being largely a voluntary activity. Individual projects have an almost inevitable tendency to drift. There appears to be no obvious remedy other than the use of direct pressure.

2.2.1.2   Formative Committees

It is often the case that much of the important development work on a standard is not done within the committee that finally endorses it. This is especially true of ISO, for whom technically stable input is often provided by national bodies such as ANSI and other groups such as ECMA and CCITT. When this situation occurs the effective input that the endorsing committee provides is often limited to editorial and cosmetic alterations.

2.2.1.3   ISO

The principal objective of ISO is to promote the development of standards world-wide with a view to facilitating the international exchange of goods and services, and to develop co-operation in the sphere of intellectual, scientific, technological and economic activity. Bearing these things in mind ISO can

- take action to facilitate co-ordination and unification of national standards and issue necessary recommendations to member bodies for this purpose;

- publish International Standards;

- encourage the development of new standards having common requirements for use in the national or international arena;

- arrange for the exchange of information regarding work of its member
  bodies and technical committees; and

- co-operate with other international organisations interested in related
  matters, particularly by undertaking at their request studies relating to
  standardisation projects.

2.2.2 The ISO/IEC Joint Technical Committee on Information Technology

In the early 1960s ISO identified a need for technical committees to deal with
computers and information processing. This resulted in the inception of ISO/
TC95 (Technical Committee 95) concerned with office machines and ISO/
TC97 concerned with computers and information processing. These two
technical committees merged at the beginning of the 1980s into ISO/TC97. In
1987 the ISO and IEC Councils established ISO/IEC JTC1 (Joint Technical
Committee 1), the first technical committee formed jointly by two principal
international standards organisations. JTC1 is concerned with IT. Its original
components were ISO/TC97 (Information Technology) with all of its subcom-
mittees, IEC/TC83 (Information Technology Equipment) and IEC/SC47B
(Microprocessor Systems). The Joint Technical Committee, in addition to
having a chairman, has a secretariat which is a member body appointed by the

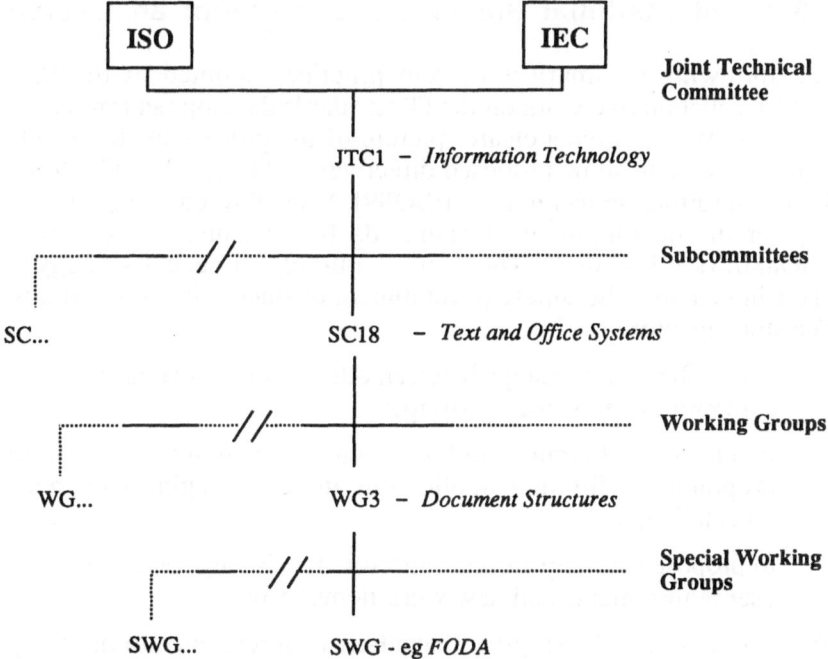

Figure 1. The ISO/IEC Joint Committee hierarchy.

councils. The constitutions of the ISO and IEC order the Joint Technical Committee secretariat to maintain strict neutrality and to differentiate carefully between its interests as a member body and its capacity as secretariat. The secretariat holds responsibility for the satisfactory conduct of the work of the Joint Technical Committee and reports annually to the Councils on the results achieved. Figure 1 shows the ISO/IEC joint committee structure graphically.

In 1988 a new era in co-operation between the largest and the most influential standards organisations reached fruition. ISO, the IEC and CCITT produced a joint 'Informal guide' [ISO88a] for co-operation between themselves, in which open sharing of information and the goodwill of each collaborator is the basis of the co-operation. The area addressed by this collaboration is information technology, and it proved to be very effective for the following projects:

- open systems interconnection (OSI) — the X.200-series;

- message handling systems — the X.400-series;

- directories — the X.500-series; and

- document architecture — the T.410-series.

2.3   The Standards Development Process

2.3.1   International Standards Generation: an Overview

The following summarises current practices adopted in the ISO/IEC and CCITT collaborative work on the IT standards development process.

In an effort to give a clearer picture of the process of the development of standards we cite some proposed directives of JTC1/SC18 which works in the field of information technology [ISO89]. Special reference is given to a strategy for the development of standards for text and office systems (TOS) [ISO88b] (see Figure 2). The primary purpose of such a strategy is to assist JTC1 in planning the timely development of International Standards for TOS. The strategy aims

- to establish relationships between other relevant standards bodies and ISO committees and working groups;

- to ensure coherence and efficiency by avoiding conflicting work programmes, limiting duplication and encouraging user readable documentation; and

- to propose a timely programme for developing technical contributions, user requirements and new work items (NWIs).

The procedure for developing a standard with reference to user requirements follows a well defined three-fold model. The stages of this model are

- the initial identification of user requirements;

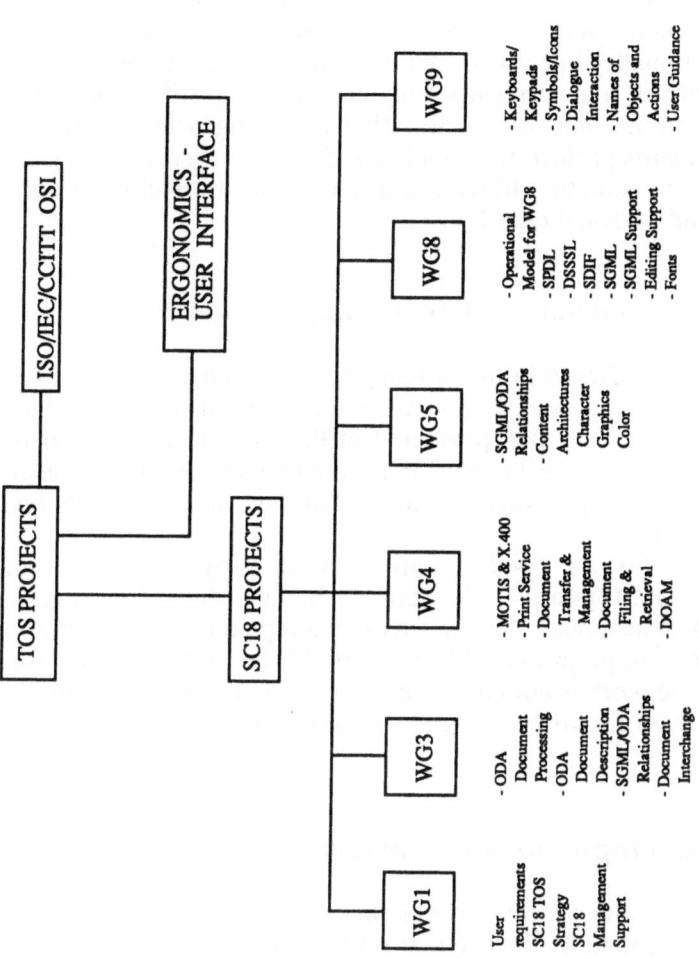

Figure 2. The proposed SC18 projects model.

- the advancement of user requirements as the International Standard develops; and

- the review of the developing International Standard.

2.3.1.1 Identification of User Requirements

The primary stage of the model calls for the gathering of information in terms of user requirements and the expression of a need for standardisation in terms of global functionality in a given area. However, this phase in the development process should still maintain sufficient generality to justify standardisation for typical applications. All this information gathering occurs early in the life cycle of a standards project. It is emphasized that the user requirements may be derived from any source, although the main ones are technical committees, user groups and personal contributions.

2.3.1.2 Advancement of User Requirements

The information gathered in the primary stage is then collated, examined and re-examined, resulting in a clear, concise statement of the user requirements. These requirements are then presented in the form of a proposal for a new work item (NWI). The NWI takes into account a classification of users and the applicability of the requirements to more than one standards area, i.e. generic user requirements.

A proposal for an NWI, complete with projected target dates for completion, is put forward to the national bodies (those ISO members with voting rights). If accepted, the NWI will be adopted and given an appropriate project number (e.g. project JTC1 18.10.12 is FODA). This number is retained until the work is completed or discontinued. Any proposals to add new work to a programme of ongoing work is decided by voting through letter-ballots.

2.3.1.3 Development and Review

The final stage in the process checks that the draft standard fulfils both the particular requirement of the original NWI proposal and the general requirements for standards documents. Conformance clauses within the draft standard should be closely scrutinised during this phase because of the complexities inherent in the development of IT standards. Furthermore, the way in which the information is presented should allow for easy comprehension by those readers who are most likely not to be conversant with standards terminology. Accordingly, the introduction, scope, field of application, references and general concepts need to be carefully completed and edited. This is also useful in the multilingual International Standards development community; clear English text facilitates translation and hence allows for wider dissemination of the standard and greater user involvement. In conclusion, the final standards documentation should satisfy those well delineated user requirements initially identified in the primary stage of development.

Priorities for each subcommittee are set on which timetables and target dates are required. The specific stages allocated to the target dates are

- the registration of a first Draft Proposal (DP) and any subsequent DPs;

- the submission of text for processing as a Draft International Standard (DIS); and

- the completion of the DIS text for publication as an International Standard (IS).

All this can take a long time; for example, the latest version of the COBOL standard took ten years to reach final approval and publication.

2.3.2   An Analogy with the Software Development Process

There are notable similarities between the processes of software development and standards development, which can be helpful in understanding and interpreting the latter. The so-called 'software development life-cycle' model is well known. It starts with requirements specification, a statement of what the software must do, rather than how it should do it. The next phase is architectural design, in which the system is described in terms of co-operating entities whose function and interrelation are defined. Detailed design then determines exactly how the functions of the principal entities are to be coded. Coded modules can then be integrated to form the architectural entities, which are then integrated to form the whole system. Each stage of integration must be preceded by testing to ensure that the items to be integrated all work according to their specifications.

Consider the STARTS model of the software life-cycle, as represented in the popular 'V' diagram [NCC87] (see Figure 3). In this model one can easily see why some software systems contain serious errors when they go live. Minor errors in coding can be found by testing as soon as coded modules have been produced. More serious design errors can at least be found by testing after module integration. But errors in the original requirements specification, if they are found by testing at all, will only be found at the very last stage. This is why errors made early in the development process may be detected only when it is too late to correct them.

In the analogous 'standards development life-cycle' the requirements analysis stage arises through observing a range of existing systems and their use and identifying the scope of a new standard. The 'specification' stage consists of work items—brief descriptions of what will be produced—being raised in standards bodies. There then, in general, follows a protracted production phase in which the standard is actually developed and written, followed generally by an even more protracted 'testing' phase in which the standard is edged towards acceptance through the various levels of standards bodies. 'Service' involves the development of implementations and conformance testing, and maintenance follows in the form of the standards review process.

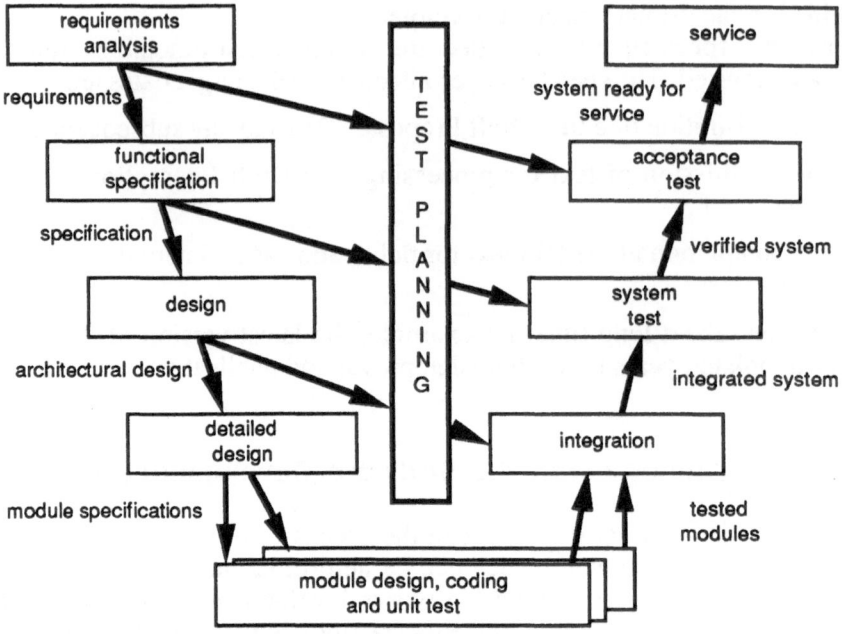

Figure 3. The STARTS model of the software life-cycle.

The analogy between software development and standards development is not exact but is close enough to enable the quality of standards to be understood in terms of more familiar ideas. The remark, for example, that errors made early in the development process may only be detected very late on in the process applies equally well to standards development as to software development.

2.4 The Quality of Standards

In engineering, quality means fitness for purpose. A standard, like a software system, can fail to help the customer or user in several ways. It may

- fail to serve a useful purpose;
- be difficult to use;
- be incompatible with other standards;
- be difficult to maintain; or
- malfunction.

Each of these defects is elaborated below.

2.4.1 Failure to Serve a Useful Purpose

Consider a consumer who has purchased software and hardware claiming to conform to some standard at a key interface. However, when connected through the interface to other conforming systems it fails to interoperate. The problem may not be that the hardware and software fail to conform to the standard but may rather be due to the standard itself. For example, this might allow variant features to be included in conforming implementations in ways which affect the invariant constructs, so that different conforming implementations may be mutually incompatible.

An example of this occurred in the early ANSI COBOL standards, which permitted two different levels of implementation of each of several separate functional areas of the language. Over one hundred thousand different variants could be claimed as conforming to the standard! Some other programming language standards have also been technically ambiguous and led to incompatibilities between compilers each claiming conformance to the same standard.

Such a situation arises through a failure to determine the true requirements of the users. In software development these requirements should be confirmed by reference to the users through frequent communication during analysis, and through some final validation process. In standards development, however, the process of identifying the potential users and discerning their needs is much more akin to product development and market research, and is very problematical.

2.4.2 Difficulty of Use

A standard may be imprecisely formulated or ambiguous, or may simply intentionally leave certain matters open to be resolved nationally or between pairs of users. Conformance cannot then be demonstrated or proved, or if proven may be worthless since it guarantees nothing.

It is clear that for ease of use the format, notations and style of the standard are critical. Size is also an important factor; a manual of several hundred pages acts as a major deterrent to the use of a standard.

There have been several attempts to define graphical notations for time-sequence diagrams in data communication standards. Unfortunately, modern systems are so complex that the notation is highly unwieldy. In this case difficulty of use has actually prevented the adoption of such standards. Process standards in particular can become very lengthy.

2.4.3 Incompatibility with Other Standards

If developed in isolation, standards will fail to integrate with one another. In order to prevent this they must be perceived as part of a system of standards. Examples of such systems of standards are the OSI networking standards and the process standards within a quality manual for software development. A typical failure of the process standards might be a design method that does not fit with the prescribed programming language, or a change control method that does not integrate with the project planning and control standard.

A method of ensuring an integrated set of standards is to develop a **reference model**, which defines the scope and common concepts of a set of standards and provides a framework for their comparison. A reference model may also be used to ensure the completeness of coverage of the standards in the set. An example is the IEEE Software Engineering Standards Taxonomy (ANSI/IEEE 729).

2.4.4 Difficulty of Maintenance

The requirements for standards change, so they need to be updated. As with software, the maintenance of a standard implies both correction and change. The principles of structured software design are well known, a technique which attempts to ensure that changes are in general localised. The design documentation should refer to the alternatives considered and the reasons for their rejection. The latter point is especially helpful in the case of standards development, where maintenance difficulties may be eased if the rationale for the selection or rejection of particular options considered during analysis and production is retained.

2.4.5 Malfunction

One can regard software malfunction as a failure to perform as expected. The causes of this can be diverse: the user may have failed to understand correctly the specification of the software; the software may be being used for the wrong purpose or outside its working limits; or the software may not meet its specification (i.e. it contains errors).

While a standard does not 'perform' in the same sense as software, it may nevertheless be misunderstood or misused or contain errors. Thus the concept of malfunctioning does have a sensible analogy for standards.

An example of such an 'error' in a standard would be a semantic indeterminacy whereby two different, apparently conforming implementations can be generated which are mutually incompatible.

3.
Formal Methods: the Background

3.1 What Are Formal Methods?

Contemporary *formal methods* either consist of, or incorporate, a *formal description technique* (FDT) which is a technique for the production of precise *specifications*. An FDT is based upon a symbolic notation (its *metalanguage*, otherwise known as a *formal specification language* (FSL)) which uses rigorous and unambiguous rules both with respect to developing expressions in the language (its *syntax*) and interpreting the meaning of these expressions (its *semantics*). A natural language description, on the other hand, is an example of an informal description technique. It is made imprecise through the presence of ambiguities and idioms.

Some formal methods, known as *formal development methods* (FDMs), also incorporate methods for undertaking 'verified design', i.e. they provide the mathematical apparatus whereby design steps may be checked against the specification and shown to satisfy it.

For a more complete and rigorous set of definitions the reader is referred to the glossary of terms (Appendix *B*).

Formal methods may be used in the development and specification of an international standard or parts thereof. A consequence of the formal style of expression is that the properties of standards thus specified can be demonstrated by mathematical reasoning about those constructions without having to build and test a real implementation of the standard. Sometimes properties can be determined by automated analysis techniques. The analysis of specifications is a major benefit of formal methods. The early detection of potential design errors can save large correction costs.

A formal specification may be accompanied by a (possibly extensive) natural language commentary, just as a natural language specification may be supplemented with expressions in symbolic notations.

Currently available formal methods have differing origins, theoretical bases, notational styles, and areas of application. They lead to specifications of differing form and content. Since specifications are the basis of quality procedures, the use of any particular formal method will strongly influence the elements of a corresponding quality system.

The remainder of this chapter surveys in outline several formal methods used in software specification. These methods are particularly appropriate for application in the specification of software-related standards. A knowledge of formal methods terminology is assumed in the text, but cross-references (indicated by italicised words) are also given to the glossary of terms (Appendix *B*). Names of languages and named documented methods are indicated by bold type on first occurrence; they are described later in the section.

3.2 A Survey of Formal Methods

Methods to be employed in the specification of software may be placed on the following axes:

- formal—semi-formal—informal;

- textual (verbal/word-based)—graphic (iconic/symbolic).

A further distinction may be made between methods for specifying sequential software and those for specifying concurrent software.

Making use of such a taxonomy, the remainder of this section presents an annotated bibliography covering the definition and usage of particular formal methods which have been, and are being, employed in the specification of software generally. In some cases they have also been used in the specification of software standards (see later chapters). Where tools supporting a formal method are known to exist, details are given. The final sub-section covers, for the purposes of comparison, some less formal methods and notations.

3.2.1 FDTs and FSLs for Sequential Software

Hoare's survey and tutorial [Hoa87] discusses various types of FDT and FSL derived from mathematics including *logic*, *algebra* and *functions*. He illustrates the role of *propositional calculus* in the formalisation of requirements and *predicate calculus* in more detailed specification. He then proceeds to show how an algebraic specification and a functional approach improve efficiency. The translation to a *procedural* language gives the very highest efficiency, but requires the replacement of *conjunction* by sequential composition, and thus imposes on the programmer the necessity of planning for the use and re-use of resources by means of sequential composition. The relationship between these types of FDT is summarised in Figure 4.

Specific formal methods discussed by Hoare include **Z**, **Prolog**, functional languages and the use of asserted *pre-conditions* and *post-conditions*. Z has been classed as a 'model-based' approach to specification. Other model-based approaches include **VDM**, **me too**, **HOS** and **Gist**. These may be contrasted with 'property-oriented' approaches: for example, algebraic specification languages such as **Clear** and **OBJ**, **ACT ONE** and **ACT TWO**, **CIP-L** and **LPG**. A brief history and evaluation of the potential of algebraic specification within ESPRIT is given by Ehrig and Pepper [Ehr88]. The **Larch** specification language shows evidence of both these approaches [Coh86].

Descriptions of these and some other FDTs follow. Model-based and property-oriented techniques are grouped together but otherwise the ordering is without significance.

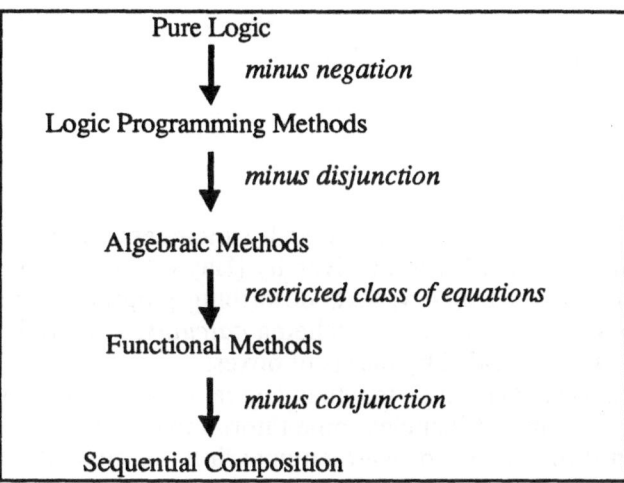

Figure 4. The relationship between various types of FDT for sequential software, after Hoare. The direction of the arrows is that of improved efficiency.

3.2.1.1   VDM (Vienna Development Method)

VDM is a software specification and production method with three components: a notation for expressing software specification, design and development; an inference system for constructing formal proofs of correctness; and a methodological framework for developing software from a specification in a formally verifiable manner. An early introduction to VDM is given by Bjørner and Jones [Bjø82]; this book also contains a number of examples. The program development aspects of VDM are described in [Jon80]. A more recent sequel places considerable emphasis on the construction of formal proofs of correctness [Jon86].

The metalanguage of VDM is known as **VDM-SL** ('VDM specification language') or **Meta-IV**. It derives from **VDL** ('Vienna Definition Language') which was used to define the programming language PL/I. It has undergone many changes during the lifetime of VDM and several 'dialects' are currently used. A BSI Panel (IST/5/50) is, however, working to produce a standard for VDM-SL [And88]. The *abstract syntax* and *concrete syntax* will themselves be formally expressed in VDM-SL. A formal semantic definition will be based on the abstract syntax.

A technical advisory group established by the CEC, 'VDM-Europe', meets regularly to discuss issues pertinent to VDM, and organises symposia at eighteen-month intervals [Bjø87; Blo88]. Various tools supporting VDM have been and are being developed [e.g. Cot85; Jon88]; it has been used within the ESPRIT VIP project to specify the PCTE [Mid88; Mid89]. VDM has been used in attempts to derive a formal specification of the programming languages PL/I [Bek74], Pascal [And82] and Ada [Bjø80] as well as parts of the graphics standard GKS (see Section 4.4). The RAISE project [Nie89] is developing a new software development method, associated specification language, and support tools, by extending VDM. RAISE aims to enable the stepwise development of concurrent as well as sequential software.

3.2.1.2   Z

Z is a specification method developed by members of the Programming Research Group (PRG) at Oxford University [Hay87]. It uses a combination of logic and elementary *set theory*; texts describing programs are structured by means of **schemas**, together with a schema *calculus*. A graphical represent-ation for schemas is provided by means of boxes.

Hayes' book [Hay87] brings together several papers and reports pertaining to Z in a single volume. It includes some tutorial material, but concentrates on case studies in three areas: software engineering, distributed computing and transaction processing.

A syntax for Z is given by King *et al.* [Kin86] and a formal semantics can be found in Spivey's books [Spi88a; Spi88b]. Other useful references on Z can be found in various PRG publications [Abr80a; Suf86] and books on specification [Abr80b; Coh86]. A recent development of Z has been a variant addressing the earliest phases of the design process, i.e. systems architecture, characterised as **Object-Oriented Subsystem Specification** by its proposers [Sch86]. Tools to support the editing of Z specifications have been developed as part of the FORSITE Project (Alvey Project No. 065).

3.2.1.3   me too

The **me too** specification language is a variant of VDM which has been pro-vided with the operational semantics of the LispKit [Hen84]. Thus **me too** specifications may be executed.

3.2.1.4   HOS and AXES

HOS ('Higher Order Software') is an FDT developed by Hamilton and Zeldin [Ham76a; Ham76b] and popularised by James Martin [Mar85a]. Specification within HOS is accomplished using the algebraic language **AXES**. Examples of the use of AXES have been published by the company which markets HOS [e.g. Hac79].

3.2.1.5   Gist

Wile and his colleagues at the University of Southern California have devel-oped Gist, which is based on operational modelling over relational databases [Gol80; Wil82]. The operational base of Gist allows executable specifications.

3.2.1.6   Clear

An informal introduction to Clear has been provided by Burstall and Goguen [Bur81]. An account which emphasises the structuring aspect of Clear can be found in an earlier paper [Bur77]. In this paper, Burstall and Goguen speculate that while Clear is intended as a tool for program specification, it could also be used to represent knowledge. The semantics of Clear are given in [Bur80a].

3.2.1.7   OBJ

The Clear language has inspired aspects of OBJ. An introduction to OBJ can be found in Goguen and Tardo [Gog79].

A tool supporting OBJ, **ObjEx**, has been developed at UMIST [Col87]. This tool provides both animation and execution of OBJ specifications.

3.2.1.8   ACT ONE and ACT TWO

The algebraic specification language ACT ONE defined by the ACT-group in Berlin [Ehr82; Ehr83; Ehr85] was mainly influenced by a simpler specification language, **LOOK**, developed by Zilles et al. [Zil82]. The specification language **LOTOS** (see Section 3.2.2) uses ACT ONE for the representation of data and value expressions. ACT TWO is a more recent development which explicitly separates the specification of a module interface from the specification of its implementation [Ehr86].

3.2.1.9   CIP-L

The Computer-Aided Intuition-Guided Programming (CIP) group at the Technical University of Munich has developed the CIP-L language to describe software from initial requirements to code optimizations [Bro84]. CIP-L is supported by a comprehensive support environment, CIP-S [Bra82]. The CIP-S system has itself been described in CIP-L.

3.2.1.10 LPG

LPG ('Language for Generic Programming') is an algebraic specification language developed by Bert and Echahed [Ber83; Ber86]. Underlying LPG is the institution of *Horn clause* logic with equality; thus, some parts of LPG specifications may be executed.

LPG has been used in the specification of the UNIX file system [Dec88].

3.2.1.11 Larch

An informal account of Larch used in combination with **CLU** is given by Liskov and Guttag [Lis86]. Tutorials have been provided by Guttag et al. [Gut85a;

Gut85b]. An experimental toolset supporting Larch has been developed at the University of Nancy [Les84].

3.2.1.12 Logic Languages—the Prolog Family

The **Prolog** language was originally developed by Colmerauer *et al.* at Marseilles; further development of Prolog in the UK has been centred at Edinburgh University and Imperial College, London. Variants of Prolog developed in the UK include **PARLOG** [Cla83] and **Perlog** [Mof88]; and in Hungary, **MPROLOG** [Ben80] and **T-PROLOG** [San82]. Use of this language for specification has been noted by Kowalski [Kow85]. A full account of logic programming and Prolog is given by Clocksin [Clo84]; together with Mellish, he has also written an introductory textbook on Prolog [Clo81].

IMCL (the Information Modelling by Composition Language) was developed by Durchholz and Richter [Ric88]. A subset of IMCL which is used in the specification of ODA (see Section 4.3.2 below) will soon appear as an International Standard (ISO 8613-10). This subset has an executable semantics in Prolog [Kar88].

3.2.1.13 Functional Languages

Functional languages are based on the *lambda calculus* developed by Alonzo Church [Chu36]. Another influence on the development of functional languages has been *Kleene recursion equations* [Kle36]. Various functional languages have been advocated for describing software; most of these are based on *recursion equations*. Functional languages include the following: **LISP** [McC60], **ML** [Gor79a, Wik87], **Hope** [Bur80b], **Miranda** [Tur85] and **FP** [Bac78]. A collection of introductory material on functional languages and associated tools can be found in Eisenbach [Eis87]. A good survey of functional programming has been provided by Darlington *et al.* [Dar82; Dar84]. Turner has demonstrated how functional languages may be regarded as specification languages [Tur85].

3.2.2 FDTs and FSLs for Concurrent Software

The representation of *finite-state machines* (FSMs) through state transition tables and diagrams is a development contemporary with Chomsky's development of grammars to describe formal languages and their application to describe the syntax of Algol 60 known as *Backus Naur Form* (BNF). A classic introductory text covering the theory of finite-state machines is Minsky's 'Computation: Finite and Infinite Machines' [Min67]. Descriptive methods for real-time systems based on FSM modelling include the CCITT's **SDL** ('Specification and Description Language') (CCITT Z.100-Z.104), **RSL** ('Requirements Statement Language') [Alf77; Bel77] and **RTRL** ('Real-Time Requirements Language') [Tay80]. A discussion of constructs for describing time constraints in real-time systems illustrated by examples in RTRL can be found in Dasarathy [Das85].

Finite-state modelling of systems provides a means of specification, design, verification and systematic testing for communication systems engineers; however, this method is not easily extended to describe complex communications systems. To overcome these difficulties, 'process algebras' were developed providing an algebraic means of expressing concurrency and a form of inferential reasoning about system behaviour; these include Milner's **CCS** (*'Calculus of Communicating Systems'*) [Mil80] and **SCCS** ('Synchronous CCS'), Hoare's **CSP** (*'Communicating Sequential Processes'*) [Hoa85a], and **LOTOS** (*'Language of Temporal Ordering Specification'*) (ISO 8807) based on CCS. The **PEEP** ('Pictorial Exposition of Executing Programs') tool developed by Bustard *et al.* supports the pictorial animation of specifications of concurrent systems in CSP, CCS, SDL and LOTOS [Bus88].

Five techniques with varying degrees of formality are currently used in communication standards, and have themselves been standardised. LOTOS is the only one with fully formal semantics; the others are **Estelle** ('Extended Finite State Machine Language'), **SDL** ('Specification and Description Language'), **ASN.1** ('Abstract Syntax Notation—One') and **TTCN** ('Tree and Tabular Combined Notation'). A report produced as part of a CEC RACE project provides a critical evaluation of LOTOS, Estelle and SDL [SPE86]. Guidelines on the usage of these three FDTs are being formulated by ISO (ISO 10167).

Petri nets, discussed below under 'Graphical Formalisms', can also be classed as a process algebra although they are in practice used simply to describe the structure of concurrent systems in conjunction with analysis tools to establish required properties [Rea88]. The **Gypsy** system based on axiomatic proof theory also provides for the description of concurrency [Coh86]. Extensions to VDM to handle concurrency have been proposed by Jones [Jon83].

3.2.2.1   LOTOS

LOTOS (ISO 8807) is a mathematically-defined FDT, developed from a body of theory based on CCS and CSP. ACT ONE is used for the description of *abstract data types*. The well-defined mathematical foundation of LOTOS provides a basis for analysis and for the development of support tools, which include simulators, compilers, and test sequence generators [Tur87; Bol88].

The basic constructs of LOTOS allow modelling of sequencing, choice, concurrency and non-determinism in an entirely unambiguous way. LOTOS also permits modelling of synchronous or asynchronous communication. LOTOS may be used to specify exactly the allowed behaviours of a system, i.e. the set of all behaviours which may be observed of a conforming implementation. Furthermore, LOTOS permits the description of allowed behaviours without describing how they may be achieved, or by describing particular mechanisms which achieve the required behaviour.

3.2.2.2   *Estelle*

Estelle (ISO 9074) is a specification language, partly formally defined, for describing distributed or concurrent processing systems, in particular those which implement OSI services and protocols [Bud87]. The language is based on widely used and accepted concepts of communicating, non-deterministic, finite state machines. An Estelle specification defines a system of hierarchically-structured state machines. The machines communicate by exchanging messages through bi-directional channels connecting their communication ports. These messages are queued at either end of the channel.

Estelle is a modification and extension to Pascal where program-level constructs are replaced by constructs to define finite-state modules exchanging queued messages. Thus familiarity with Pascal makes Estelle specifications easily readable. The use of Pascal is, however, restricted so as to avoid difficulties of verification. A formal semantics is given only for the extensions.

In addition to allowing the modelling of communication between the state machines of a specified system, Estelle language mechanisms permit dynamic development of the system configuration.

3.2.2.3   *SDL*

SDL (CCITT Z.100-Z.104) is based on an extended finite state machine model, supplemented by capabilities for abstract data types. Its linguistic form resembles Pascal with various extensions to express system modularisation and communication. As originally conceived, SDL had no formal semantics and did not support formal specification or checking to any great extent. However, a formal semantics is now under development.

SDL provides constructs to represent structures, behaviours, interfaces and communication links [Sar87]. In addition, it provides constructs for *abstraction*, module encapsulation, and refinement. All of these constructs were designed to assist the representation of a variety of telecommunications system specifications, including aspects of services and protocols. SDL is widely used in the telecommunications community, and is supported by a variety of tools, some of which are generally available.

3.2.2.4   *ASN.1*

ASN.1 (ISO 8824; ISO 8825) is defined in alignment with CCITT Recommendation X.409. It is intended for the specification of data structures and their encoding for communication purposes. Though not given an explicit mathematical definition, ASN.1 is nevertheless clearly defined and its semantics could be formalised without technical difficulty. The main limitation of ASN.1 is that it does not deal with sequential aspects of system behaviour.

3.2.2.5 TTCN

TTCN (ISO 9646) is intended for the specification of abstract conformance tests. TTCN uses state-transition methods for defining sequential behaviour but permits the use of ad hoc notation for data entities. It is thus somewhat complementary to ASN.1, the latter being often used with TTCN for data description purposes. No formal semantics is given in the defining document.

3.2.2.6 Gypsy

Gypsy, developed at the University of Texas at Austin [Amb86], is a language to support the specification, coding and verification of systems software with particular emphasis on communications software. Applications of Gypsy are discussed in Good *et al.* [Goo79] and Cheheyl *et al.* [Che81]. Gypsy is supported by an extensive toolset.

3.2.3 Graphical Formalisms

3.2.3.1 Petri Nets

Petri nets have been used to describe causal relationships between events in asynchronous processes [Pet62]. They provide a method for modelling systems of interacting concurrent components. An introduction to Petri nets and their applications is given by Peterson [Pet81]; a more formal introduction can be found in Reisig [Rei85]. The use of Petri nets as a formal language for knowledge representation has been recently proposed by Fidelak [Fid86]. A scheme for software system design representation and analysis based on the Petri net formalism has been described by Varadharajan and Baker [Var87].

Design methods based on nets include **SARA** ('System Architect's Apprentice') [Cam78] and **GALILEO**. Toolsets supporting net-theoretic specification include tools supporting SARA, GALILEO and **SREM** ('Software Requirements Engineering Methodology') [Alf80]. Nets have been used to define the PEARL programming language (DIN 66253).

3.2.3.2 Higraphs

Higraphs are a visual formalism developed recently by David Harel [Har88]. Harel reviews topological formalisms from Euler's early work on graphs and Euler circles, now better known as Venn diagrams. He shows how an extended form of graphs, the 'hypergraph'—where edges may connect more than a pair of nodes—may be combined with a modified and extended form of Euler/Venn diagrams to give what he terms higraphs. He then shows how higraphs may be applied to describe entity-relationship models, semantic and associative networks, data-flow diagrams, and finite state machines and their transitions. This article contains a formal definition of higraphs, and an extensive set of references.

A system called **STATEMATE** has been implemented to support higraph-based formalisms [ILo87, Har87].

3.2.4   Less Formal Methods and Notations

The methods and languages listed below are less formal in the sense that they lack a complete formal semantics. Typically they support structured analysis and design of systems and have an associated diagrammatic notation used to show relationships between the various entities that comprise the system, the processes that manipulate those entities and data flow between processes. Barry Böhm has characterised these methods as 'formatted', in contrast to more formal mathematical methods [Böh79].

3.2.4.1   SADT

The Structured Analysis and Design Technique (SADT) and its associated diagrammatic notation were devised by Douglas T. Ross [Ros77]. A range of tools and training supporting this technique are available.

3.2.4.2   Structured Design

De Marco, Yourdon and Constantine and others have popularised a structured design method with an associated diagrammatic notation known as Structured Design [DeM78; Mye78; You78; Gan79; Pag80].

A discussion of various approaches to systems analysis including a comparison of De Marco's data flow diagrams and Checkland's conceptual models has been given by Benyon and Skidmore [Ben87].

3.2.4.3   SSADM and LSDM

The Structured System Analysis and Design Method (SSADM) [NCC86; Dow88] was defined jointly by the UK Central Computer and Telecommunications Agency and by Learmonth and Burchett Management Systems Ltd. (LBMS). At the time of writing, LBMS market a product based on SSADM, called LSDM; it is supported by a tool, Auto-Mate Plus, also available from LBMS.

3.2.4.4   JSP and JSD

Jackson Structured Programming (JSP) is a method of program design with an associated diagrammatic notation; *Jackson System Development* (JSD) is an extension of JSP into the area of system design [Jac75; Ing79; Jac83; Cam89]. Randell [Ran86] characterises JSP as

> Jackson's scheme of requiring that the structure of file processing software be based closely on the syntactic structure of the input and output files

and JSD as

its generalization, which keys a system's structure to that of its environment.

A recent article by Newport [New88] describes the use of JSD to specify parallel processing applications.

A tool is available [Gen88] which uses knowledge-based techniques to support the construction of models from which JSD specifications are inferred. Michael Jackson Systems Ltd in the UK offer a range of supporting tools and training on these methods.

3.2.4.5   HDM and the SPECIAL Language

The hierarchical development method (HDM) is a methodology developed at SRI which has been described by Levitt *et al.* [Lev79]. The SPECIAL language has been described by Robinson and Roubine [Rob77].

3.2.4.6   Structured Analysis and Design of Real-time Systems

The application of the methods of structured design and structured analysis in the description of real-time software is surveyed by McCabe [McC85] and Gomaa [Gom84]. Gomaa is the developer of **DARTS** ('Design Approach for Real-Time Systems') [Gom84; Gom86]. The **EPOS** specification and design technique [Bie79] uses a representation scheme similar to SADT; it was developed to support the description of computer controlled real-time automation systems. Within the UK, the **MASCOT** design method ('Modular Approach to Software Construction, Operation and Testing') with its ACP ('Activity Channel Pool') diagrams has been used in the description of concurrent systems [MSA80; Bat86; Sim86]. A comprehensive account of structured development methods applied to real-time systems can be found in Ward and Mellor [War85]. Hatley and Pirbhai have developed a real-time system specification technique which integrates a finite machine structure into the classical structured analysis methods [Hat87].

3.3   Support Tools for FDTs

3.3.1   Introduction

Since formal methods are not easy to use, they depend even more than the general run of methods on effective support from integrated tools.

FDT tools are needed for writing and changing descriptions. These tools can incorporate some kind of source version-control system to keep track of different versions. Verification tools are also important: a description which is not checked for correctness loses much of its value as an exact description of a system or a standard.

FDT tools can be divided into two categories: static and dynamic. Static tools deal only with language aspects of the FDT used for a description. Into this category fall editors, formatters, syntax and static semantics checkers, teaching tools, and static report-generators which analyse the use of language constructs. Dynamic tools deal with the behaviour of the specified system. They can be used to verify whether the system will behave as required, for example whether it is free from (unwanted) deadlock or livelock. Useful tools in this area are simulators, prototype generators, and *theorem provers*. The benefit of these tools is that it is possible to experiment with a system at an early stage, thus giving confidence in its behaviour. If the description is of a system to be built, dynamic tools can help to discover misunderstandings between the client and the specifier.

FDT tools can also be used to assist in implementation and subsequently to verify whether an implementation conforms to its specification. When stepwise refinement techniques are used to progress from the specification to an implementation, verification can be carried out for each refinement step. The tools in this category include compilers, code generators, interpreters, validators, and test sequence generators. The benefit of these tools is that they help to avoid the introduction of errors during the design process.

It is in the area of tools support that the contrast between academic attitudes and industry requirements becomes most obvious. Researchers in FDTs often view tools as hindering them by limiting their freedom to create ephemeral notations appropriate to the task of the moment. According to this view, much of the work involved in using a tool or set of tools is often a time-wasting distraction from the real problem being tackled.

Industry managers, on the other hand, take the view that until a production quality toolset is available with support, with good documentation and with training for various classes of user, the FDT itself should be viewed as ephemeral and not worth the commitment of resources.

Between these extremes lie the academic who recognizes the role of tools in technology transfer and the industrial researcher who needs regularly to demonstrate progress in concrete terms. From this area emanate many tools which use rapid prototyping technology such as logic and functional programming systems. Such tools play down the role of a particular concrete syntax, facilitating experimentation with new semantic constructs without the necessity of major reworking of the toolset. These tools serve to stimulate industry interest but tend to be subject to performance limitations, poor integration of the tool components which are often taken from other research projects, the lack of commitment to a standard syntax, and the lack of any support.

3.3.2 The Nature of FDT Tools

An early tendency in FDT tools philosophy was to constrain the user right from their first interaction with the tools system so that errors were detected on input. This led to much work on syntax editors and structure editors, with preference being given to generic structure editors tailored for particular languages. Following the development of various editors, particularly for

LOTOS, it was observed that users objected strongly to being forced into a particular mode of working. Some users preferred to enter text using their usual screen editor, knowing that some of their input was incorrect or not thought out. They then called for a syntax or semantics check at a time of their choosing, having reworked their original input many times using the facilities of their favourite editor.

By contrast, and predictably given the experience with editors, virtually all users found benefit in using animation tools to explore and build confidence in the behaviour of particular parts of a specification, amenable to execution. A by-product of this enthusiasm is that specifications then tend to be written to suit the characteristics of the animation tool. Industry generally views this as a sound policy to take maximum advantage of the tools support, whereas some FDT proponents see this as confirming their view on the distortion introduced by tools, either those whose limitations impact adversely on the specifications they process or those whose seductive characteristics promote clumsy specifications by sustaining user interaction without reflection.

The question of syntax and representation runs through most of the tools support policy with, again, differing perceptions from industry and from FDT researchers. Researchers are, in the main, opposed to the use of graphical notations and would prefer proper support for mathematical notation. Industry, intending to promote uptake by people used to flow charts, prefers either graphical syntax or a choice of syntaxes with the non-graphical syntax spelling out the reserved words. The two stances are encapsulated in the slogans 'a word is worth a thousand pictures' and 'a picture is worth a thousand words'.

A compromise is frequently adopted where mathematical symbols are approximated by characters from the ASCII set.

3.3.3 Validation and Verification Tools

Tools for validation and verification include static code analysers, animators, theorem provers, transformation aids and test sequence generators. An ability to make effective use of these tools is not widespread and their usefulness depends on the area being tackled. For large formal descriptions produced retrospectively, such as those for OSI protocols and services, theorem provers seem to have limited relevance. These tools are more effectively applied to new developments where validation and verification are planned from the outset. For some FDTs, this results in the early production of specifications that are verification-oriented. Just as for animators, the characteristics of a particular verification tool may then be reflected in the formal descriptions produced with it in mind.

A common criticism of verification tools is that they are quite often not themselves verified and are, in many cases, written in non-standard languages or languages for which no conformance test suite has been defined. This is similar to the criticism that test tools are often not themselves subjected to a sufficient degree of testing. One answer to this criticism is to construct multiple versions of tools, some in languages that are semantically close to the definitions used for the FDT and some in traditional languages such as C which enable reasonable performance. For disputed results, correlation among the alternative toolsets can improve confidence and trust.

3.3.4 Tool Environments

In the longer term, much of the the tools support for FDTs may be provided within IPSEs (**Integrated Project Support Environments**). In a wider context, it is asserted that ISFs (**Information Systems Factories**) provide the essential compost without which formal methods are unlikely to flourish. It is, however, estimated that it will be well into the 1990s before an ISF demonstrator is available. In the meantime, less ambitious undertakings have demonstrated clear advantages using loosely integrated tools running on low and medium cost workstations.

3.4 A Survey of Methods and Tools: the STARTS Guide

The STARTS guide [NCC87] is one of the products of a DTI-funded programme to promote the uptake of software engineering and its support tools by United Kingdom software industries. The guide aims to document the best current practice in the development of software and its management within the UK real-time software supply industry and its major clients.

The guide describes methods and tools which support the software engineering life-cycle (see Section 2.3.2) and its practices, and are available in a fully supported form in the UK. It identifies the phases within the life-cycle to which the tools relate but reviews them by function under the following headings:

- project management;

- configuration management;

- project infrastructure and project support environments;

- requirements definition and design; and

- verification, validation and testing.

Although the guide contains a wide spectrum of methods and tools it does not claim to be exhaustive. Indeed, by only considering so-called 'mature' tools the guide does not reflect the current state of the software engineering tools market. Consequently the presence or absence of a method or tool in the guide merely acts as a baseline against which a software developer or their client can assess a proposed software engineering environment in order to identify its advantages or shortcomings against a range of alternatives. This philosophy is designed so as not to exclude the development of new methods and tools.

4.
Formal Methods in Standards: Four Case Studies

4.1 Introduction

In this section we turn to the application of formal techniques for software specification to the development and expression of standards.

Experiences in different application areas vary considerably. In the field of communicating systems, for example, the use of formal and semi-formal description techniques has been reasonably extensive and successful. Various semi-formal description techniques have been used for expressing specifications for OSI services and protocols, culminating in the FDTs **LOTOS**, **Estelle** and **SDL**. These three FDTs have been used to produce formal descriptions of many OSI and telecommunications standards such as **ODP** (Open Distributed Processing), **FTAM** (File Transfer, Access and Management), **ACSE** (Association Control Service Element), **X-25**, **ISDN** (Integrated Services Digital Network) and **Signalling Systems No. 7**.

The two main standards concerning document structures are **SGML** and **ODA**. The SGML standard uses a variety of BNF (see Section 4.2.1 below) to improve on the informality of plain text. A formal specification of ODA (**FODA**) is currently being developed within ISO/IEC as a separate, self-contained, part of the ODA standard (ISO 8613-10); this is expressed as a single formula in *first-order predicate calculus*.

Experience in the field of programming languages is different again. Until recently, no common terms of reference had emerged for the definition of programming languages with, for example, Modula-2 currently being defined formally using VDM-SL but the idea of a formal definition having been totally rejected in the case of C. Recently, ISO guidelines have been drawn up and are to be published.

Four case studies are presented below, concerning standards development in the areas of programming languages (Section 4.2), document structure (Section 4.3), graphics (Section 4.4) and communicating systems (Section 4.5).

4.2 Programming Languages

Though the need for a clear, precise, unambiguous specification of a programming language is well understood, in the area of standards this goal has yet to be achieved. Programming language standards are generally sufficiently full of ambiguities as to cause significant problems to implementers. Definers of programming language standards initially attempted to solve this problem by using formal methods to specify the syntax of the language; more recently formal methods have allowed the semantics to be specified as well. This section briefly reviews the various approaches to programming language definition and then illustrates how a particular formal approach (the denotational approach) is being used to derive a formal standard for Modula-2.

4.2.1 Overview

A compiler for a programming language is just one example of a software system. Before embarking on its construction, it is useful to have an accurate definition of the programming language. Such a definition must, in some sense, be precise: it must also be unambiguous, non-self-contradictory, complete, and (of course!) usable.

Possible languages that might be used for defining a programming language are

* a natural language such as English;

* an existing programming language whose semantics is well understood; or

* a special-purpose language.

Natural languages have a fundamental problem of ambiguity, perhaps best illustrated by considering the number of different meanings that might be ascribed to the phrase 'it's tough on the street' used in the advertisement for a French car. Ways around this have been tried: for example, the definition of the PL/I programming language was written in a stylized version of English. The resulting Standard (ISO 6522) is rather large, very brutal in its approach, and tedious to read, but does have the advantage of being accurate. However, in one sense it is arguably much closer to a formal specification than a natural language one, since it could almost automatically be translated into a mathematical definition.

A second approach is to use a compiler, written in an existing programming language, as the definition of a new programming language. The meaning of a program in the language being defined is then determined by examining the output from the compiler. While this approach can be made to work, there are some major difficulties, such as the question of which machine language will be used as the output from the compiler (or, equivalently, which hardware will be used as the basis of the definition) and the fact that the compiler may be badly written and contain machine dependencies and bugs. The fundamental problem underlying these difficulties is that a compiler necessarily contains implementation details, so that attention is focussed upon how a program will work on a particular target machine rather than upon what the program will do.

A third approach is to describe the execution of a program at a very high level. This can be achieved by 'compiling' to an abstract computer—a sort of generalisation of all machines in existence today. In order to define the compiler, a very high-level language is needed—one that allows data to be described in a very abstract fashion and concentrates on what algorithms do rather than how they should be implemented on particular machines. The language need not even be executable. A suitable language has been in existence for 3000 years—namely mathematics: it has a highly successful track record as a means of describing systems. Formal (mathematical) techniques allow a programming language to be defined with great precision. In recent years a number of mathematically based special-purpose languages have been developed specifically for defining programming languages.

Formal methods were first used to specify programming language *syntax*. Algol 60 was one of the first programming languages for which a formal definition of the language syntax was devised. The formalism for syntactic description used in the revised report on Algol 60 was proposed initially by J.W. Backus [Bac59]. The formalism consists of metalinguistic formulae which completely define all well-formed formulae allowable in the language. The semantics of Algol 60 was defined by natural language text lacking the conciseness and completeness of ***Backus-Naur Form*** (BNF), as the formalism for syntactic description came to be known.

The successful application of formal methods to the definition of syntax led to work on the formal definition of *semantics*. Although producing a formal specification of a programming language's semantics is a more complex task than defining its syntax, work in this area is well advanced, and several approaches now exist. These include the following:

- **W-Grammars** [Wij75; Cle77; McG78]. These are, roughly speaking, extensions to BNF that allow the semantics as well as the syntax to be included in the description of the language.

- **Operational Semantics** [Weg72a; Weg72b; Oll74]. The style of operational semantics describes the execution of a program on an abstract machine, an approach taken in the early definitions of PL/I and indeed in the PL/I Standard (ISO 6522). This approach does, however, have the disadvantage of insufficient abstraction.

- **Axiomatic Semantics** [Hoa69; Hoa73]. Axiomatic semantics has been used to describe small languages, but it is not clear whether it is applicable to realistic languages such as Algol, Fortran or Modula-2.

- **Attribute Grammars** [May81]. These belong to the same family of definition languages as W-grammars in that additional information is added to the concrete syntax to allow the semantics of programs to be described.

- **Denotational Semantics** [Mil76; Sto77; Gor79b; Sch88]. This approach will be described in some detail below.

A survey of work on programming language semantics can be found in Pagan's book, 'Semantics of Programming Languages: A Panoramic Primer' [Pag81]; a less comprehensive account but one which appears to have been motivated by a recognition of the need for formal definition in programming language standardisation can be found in Marcotty *et al.* [Mar76].

The formal definition of programming languages has been progressing for the last twenty years. The list of languages that have been formally defined include Ada, CHILL, Lucid, Minimal BASIC, Modula-2, Pascal, PL/I, SCHEME, Snobol, Algol 60, APL, LISP, Algol 68 and the Dijkstra family of guarded command languages. The application of formal techniques in the development of programming language standards is, however, less advanced. The proposed Modula-2 Standard is written in a formal language, as is Ada. It is noticeable that those languages that were formally defined from the outset tend to be smaller and more concise, particular examples of this being SCHEME, Lisp, APL and Algol 68. Below is a list of programming language standards projects: those using a formal method for specifying the semantics of the standard are starred.

- Ada (ISO 8652)
- Algol (ISO 1538)
- APL (ISO 8485)
- BASIC (ISO 10279)
- C (ISO 9899)
- CHILL (ISO 9496)
- Cobol (ISO 1989)

- Fortran (ISO 1539; ISO 7846)
- LISP*
- Minimal BASIC (ISO 6373)
- Modula-2*
- Pascal (ISO 7185)
- Prolog*

4.2.2 The Denotational Approach to the Formal Definition of a Programming Language

A formal definition must define a standard program and give a meaning to that standard program. This can be accomplished using mathematics as follows.

Each program written in a programming language can be thought of as defining a function F from the set of all possible inputs to the program to the set of all possible outputs (see Figure 5). Executing a program consists of presenting it with a particular input and seeing what output is produced. The definition of a programming language should allow a user to deduce what his or her program will do to a particular set of inputs. However, how a compiler or interpreter produces code to carry this out should be beyond the scope of the definition.

In order to define a programming language formally it is necessary to define a *meaning function M*. This function will take a program text and transform it into the function F mentioned above. In order to give a precise definition of F it is necessary to give a precise definition of the 'set of all possible inputs' and the 'set of all possible outputs'. This is done by constructing an abstract mathematical model of every part of the computer that is relevant to the execution of the program. This includes a model of both short- and long-term storage (i.e. the computer store and filing system). Using this model it is possible to describe the meaning of any statement in the language by describing the changes it makes to the model.

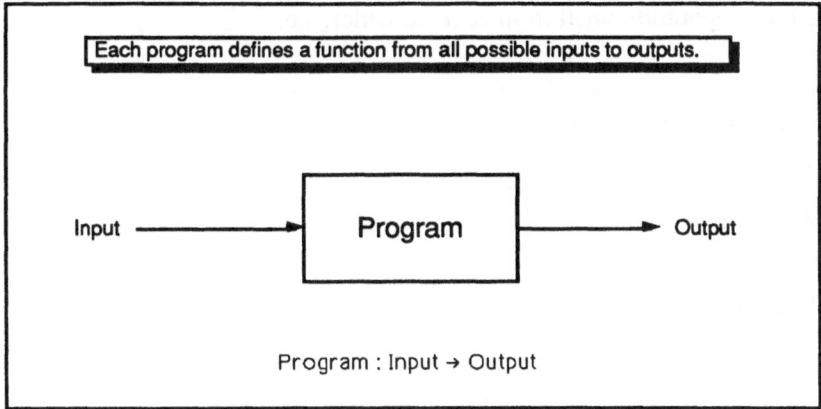

Figure 5. The meaning of a program.

Thus the function M transforms a *denotation*, i.e. a program or program fragment, into a function from input (the state of the mathematical model of the computer store and files before the fragment is 'executed') to output (the state of the model after the execution of the program or fragment). These ideas are represented mathematically as follows:

$M \llbracket \text{program} \rrbracket = F$

$F : State \rightarrow State$

$M : Denotation \rightarrow (State \rightarrow State)$

where 'State' represents the mathematical model of the computer. The set of instructions on how to build M is the formal definition of the programming language.

F is constructed from the denotation of the program using mathematically familiar tools such as functions and operations on functions. Suppose, for example, that it were necessary to give meaning to a program written in a Pascal-like language:

```
M ⟦   program x;
       var a,b : Integer;
       begin
          a:=0;
          b:=1;
          a:=a+b
       end.
    ⟧
```

The meaning of the program can be found by giving meaning to each of the declarations and statements in turn. In other words, the meaning function for the whole program is given by the meaning function applied to components of that program, combined together in order using functional *composition*. By defining a semi-colon combinator to be equivalent to functional composition but with the operands written in reverse order, i.e.

$F \,; G = G \circ F,$

the above expression is equivalent to

$M[\![\,\text{var a : Integer}\,]\!];$
$M[\![\,\text{var b : Integer}\,]\!];$
$M[\![\,\text{a:=0}\,]\!];$
$M[\![\,\text{b:=1}\,]\!];$
$M[\![\,\text{a:=a+b}\,]\!]$

The semi-colon combinator is in fact a mathematical artefact: the mathematical meaning of $F \,; G$ is the composition of G and F. Since applying $G \circ F$ is equivalent to applying F followed by G, a precise mathematical meaning has been given to the semi-colon symbol which is intuitively similar to its traditional meaning in programming languages.

The meaning of each individual statement can be given with respect to a statement pro-forma which can itself be given in terms of the syntax for small languages. For example, the meaning of the expression 'id1 + id2' can be given in terms of the meaning of 'id1' and the meaning of 'id2':

$M[\![\, id1 \; + \; id2 \,]\!] \triangleq$
    $\text{let } lo = M[\![\, id1 \,]\!] \text{ in}$
    $\text{let } ro = M[\![\, id2 \,]\!] \text{ in}$
    $lo + ro$

Once again, a programming language operator is defined in terms of the corresponding mathematical operator.

A problem remains. In a procedural language, the value of an expression depends upon the current values of the variables denoted by 'id1' and 'id2'. Thus, in order to give meaning to an expression, a mathematical model of the computer's short- and long-term storage must be added. Computer store can, for example, be modelled as

$State = \text{LOC} \rightarrow Value$

in other words a *mapping* from the set 'LOC' (an infinite set of tokens, each token modelling in some way a storage location) to the set 'Value' (modelling values which can be stored in storage locations). This abstract model of storage is far more general than a physical computer store because a location can hold not only a scalar value but also an array, record, or any structured value.

High-level languages remove the need when programming to refer to storage locations by their machine name. The programmer uses an abstraction, namely an identifier. This idea is modelled in formal definitions by having a second mapping, normally called the 'environment', which associates with each identifier the corresponding storage location:

$Env = Id \rightarrow \text{LOC}$

Thus the **state** is a model of the **store** (and, for the formal definition of real programming languages, also includes a model of the filing system) and the **environment** is a model of **variables**. (In a compiler the environment mapping is implemented as the dictionary, which associates with each identifier its location in computer store.) The meaning function M may now be understood as transforming a denotation into a function which itself maps an environment into a function from state to state (i.e. the state before execution to the state afterwards). This is represented mathematically as follows:

$M : Den \rightarrow Env \rightarrow (State \rightarrow State)$

The full meaning function for the expression 'id1 + id2' can now be derived. First, we note that the meaning of an identifier is just its corresponding storage location. Thus

$M : Id \rightarrow Env \rightarrow Value$

$M\, [\![\text{id}]\!]\rho \triangleq \rho(\text{id})$

Secondly, we define a 'contents' function which returns the contents of a storage location (it should be noted that this example language does not allow side effects to occur when an expression is evaluated, so that it only needs to access the state (store) when evaluating an expression).

$contents : \text{LOC} \rightarrow State \rightarrow Value$

$contents(\text{loc})\,\sigma \triangleq \sigma(\text{loc})$

Finally

$M : Expression \rightarrow Env \rightarrow State \rightarrow Value$

$M [\![\ id1\ +\ id2\ ]\!]\,\rho\,\sigma \triangleq$
   let $lo = M [\![\ id1\ ]\!]\,\rho$ in
   let $ro = M [\![\ id2\ ]\!]\,\rho$ in
   $contents(lo)\,\sigma + contents(ro)\,\sigma$

The meaning of the expression is given as follows: first, the environment is used to give the storage location corresponding to each of the identifiers; secondly, the state is used to find out the value stored in each location; and thirdly normal arithmetic is used to add these two results together. Thus a computer version of the addition operation has been defined in terms of the normal mathematical definition of addition.

The meanings of other statements can also be expressed in this formalism. For example, the meaning of a declaration is given by allocating an unused storage location, one that is not in the current domain of the state mapping, associating the identifier with that location in the environment, and adding that location together with the fact that it contains an undefined value to the state.

4.2.3   Formal Definitions of Real Languages

For a large programming language the formal definition is usually derived in two stages. The first checks the static semantics, i.e. whether it is possible to build the function F. In this stage it is checked, for example, that a label is not added to an integer variable. If the program passes the static semantic checks, it can then be given a meaning using dynamic semantics. The function is effectively built.

During static checking the environment maps identifiers to their type. This information is used when type checking expressions and, for example, assignment. For the dynamic semantics the environment maps an identifier to its storage location. (In the formal Modula-2 definition this is not quite true but the essence is as described. In fact, far more information is kept in the environment and this is merely a minor part.)

In order to illustrate these ideas we present an example from the formal definition of Modula-2. The language is defined by giving for each construct

*   the concrete syntax;

*   an abstract syntax equivalent—this is the concrete syntax with the punctuation removed;

*   a set of functions which check the static semantics; and

*   a set of meaning functions which defines the dynamic semantics.

The first of these is expressed in EBNF, the remainder in VDM-SL.

The example we shall consider is the 'if' statement. An 'if' statement is used to select a statement sequence for execution from a number of alternatives, depending upon the values of Boolean expressions.

The concrete syntax for the statement is

```
if statement =
    guarded statements, [ "ELSE", statement sequence ], "END" ;

guarded statements =
    "IF", Boolean expression, "THEN", statement sequence,
    { "ELSIF", Boolean expression,
    "THEN", statement sequence } ;
```

and the abstract syntax is

```
If-statement ::
        s-thens          : seq of Guarded-statement
        s-elsep          : [ Statement-sequence ]
```

```
Guarded-statement ::
        s-guard              : Expression
        s-body               : Statement-sequence
```

This expresses the essence of the 'if' statement. It comprises a sequence of guarded statements (note that this may be empty!) and an 'else' part. Each of the guarded statements in the sequence itself comprises an expression together with a statement sequence. The 'else' part either comprises a statement sequence or is void. The static semantics is given by

```
WF : If-statement → Environment → B

WF⟦mk-If-statement(thens,elsep)⟧ρ ≙
(∀mk-Guarded-statement(guard,body) ∈ elems thens ·
    WF⟦guard⟧ρ ∧
    TE⟦guard⟧ρ = Boolean-type ∧
    WF⟦body⟧ρ) ∧
    (elsep=nil ∨ WF⟦elsep⟧ρ)
```

The well-formedness conditions state that

(i)   each of the guarded statement components should be well-formed;

(ii)   the type (i.e. the result) of each guard expression should be Boolean; and

(iii)   if the 'else' part is present it should also be well formed.

The dynamic semantics of the statement is given by a recursive function:

```
M : If-statement → Environment

M⟦mk-If-statement(thens,elsep)⟧ρ ≙
if thens = [] then
    execute-else-statements(elsep)ρ
else
    let mk-Guarded-statement(guard,body)=hd thens in
    def value : M⟦guard⟧ρ ;
    if value then
            M⟦body⟧ρ
    else
            M⟦mk-If-statement(tl thens,elsep)⟧ρ
```

This part of the formal description describes the 'execution' of the statement. It states the following:

•   If there are no elements in the sequence of guarded statements then the 'else' part of the 'if' statement (if present) is executed.

- If on the other hand there *are* elements in the sequence of guarded statements, then the Boolean expression of the first guarded statement in the sequence is evaluated. If the result is 'true', then the corresponding statement sequence is executed. If the result is 'false', then the execution of the 'if' statement is the same as that of the 'if' statement produced when the first element in the the sequence of guarded statements is removed.

An English language description of the execution of the 'if' statement (based on the proposed Modula-2 Standard) is:

> The Boolean expressions of the sequence of guarded statements are evaluated in the order they occur until one of the Boolean expressions yields true; and then the associated statement sequence is executed. If all the Boolean expressions evaluate to false, the statement sequence of the ELSE clause (if present) is executed. An if statement denotes no action if all the Boolean expressions evaluate to the value false and there is no ELSE clause. Note that the evaluation of any of the Boolean expressions could produce a transformation of the program state, i.e. have a side-effect.

Note that in the definition we should really have written

```
M : If-statement → Environment → State → State
```

However, since the function from state to state occurs for all constructs, and can be taken as given, it is conventional to omit it and hence reduce cluttering in the definition.

4.2.4   Discussion

One of the problems in using formal methods to define a programming language, as is obvious even from the simple example above, is that they are difficult to read.

A more subtle problem is that a formal specification of a programming language is, in one sense, *too* accurate. Difficult issues and interactions between language features cannot be avoided; they must be investigated and solved. Typically, when writing an English specification for a programming language, these tricky interactions are avoided. This is not because the writers of the language description are deliberately trying to do so, but because there are too many interactions to be described in English and there is no model within which to investigate them. As a result, they tend not to be discovered. It is not possible to avoid contentious issues when using a formal description technique. An early draft of the Minimal BASIC standard had at least six different interpretations of the FOR loop. At one time the reason given for this was that there were at least six different implementations, all of which needed to be 'standard'!

The principal advantage of formal techniques is that they result in much greater accuracy. Discussion of difficult language features is provoked and solutions to these problems can be found. In all the programming languages that have been formally defined, formal methods have improved their definitions, problems in interpretation have been resolved, and because of this better design decisions have been made.

In the short term at least, it seems unrealistic to expect a formal definition to be accessible to the average programmer. However, we could expect compiler writers and book authors to read them in order to find out exactly what they are trying to implement or describe. The onus would be upon these professionals to acquire the skills necessary to understand a formal language description and to translate it into a form accessible to the average programmer.

4.3   Document Structure

This section examines two standards concerning document structures, the Standard Generalised Markup Language, SGML (ISO 8879) and the Office Document Architecture, ODA (ISO 8613; CCITT T.410 Series of Recommendations).

The first part, on SGML, contains an introduction to the subject matter, applications and readership of the standard. These raise a number of questions concerning such standards, with particular attention to appropriate use of formal notation.

The second part, on ODA, summarises the concepts behind ODA and the envisaged needs for a formal specification of this standard (FODA). A historical view is given of the development of FODA, in addition to an overview of its definition and uses, and future developments in the formal specification of ODA are discussed.

Further material on SGML is available in the Bulletin of the SGML Users' Group; see also [Bry88] and [Smi88]. Further material on ODA is referenced in the text.

4.3.1   The Standard Generalised Markup Language (SGML)

4.3.1.1   What is SGML?

SGML became an International Standard late in 1986 (ISO 8879). The name 'Standard Generalised Markup Language' is indicative. The standard's editor and main author was employed by IBM in the USA, and had worked on computer systems for producing documents (mainly for technical documentation) for many years. The UK expert panel was very active in ensuring that the standard did not have unnecessary limitations, particularly taking into account

- the production of documents to high typographic quality,

- European languages,

- currently available equipment, and

- the need for supplier- and device-independence.

The terms **Generalised Markup** and **Generic Coding** are both used for the concept at the heart of the SGML standard, and both terms are also used for other closely related but different concepts.

The intended meaning in the context of SGML is a system-independent means of marking up the text of a document, describing its content (e.g. chapter, heading, paragraph, list item) rather than its typographic features (e.g. new page, 14pt Times bold, 3ems indent, italic). SGML was intended by its developers principally as a public-domain standard for Generalised Markup. SGML does **not** (and was never intended to) provide standard copymarks for use in marking up documents (along the lines of ASPIC) [BPI89].

The SGML standard does not describe a language in which to encode documents. Rather, it gives a *metalanguage*—an *abstract syntax* for describing the character set and syntax of encoded documents, together with a default *concrete syntax* in which to code such descriptions. This concrete syntax is a useful sample character set with commonly used defaults for the markup delimiters etc.

The aim of the standard is not to restrict the kinds of document which can be handled but rather to provide a means whereby many different kinds of document, including all those currently produced by the publishing and technical documentation industries, can be coded. It allows SGML-coded documents to be in a wide variety of character sets and coding conventions to suit different devices, different kinds of documents, and different system requirements.

In the printing and publishing industry, the stages in the production of a document are usually handled by different companies or departments. In addition, the life of a document (e.g. over successive revisions of a textbook or manual) is often longer than the life of any particular system used to print it, and often longer than the lives of subcontracting companies. These factors lead to a need for a straightforward means of passing coded documents unambiguously between systems over space and time. SGML addresses this requirement for the raw text of documents, independent of page layout, hyphenation etc. Other standards are in preparation which address this requirement for paginated documents.

SGML is understood by an SGML parser, which takes the DTD (Document Type Definition—a formal description of the document character set and allowed structures) of a coded document, and can then process the document text in accordance with its coded structure. The subsequent processing of the text is of no concern here—or to the SGML standard. Typically, but not necessarily, an SGML parser is part of a computer system producing printed documents, or allowing the text to be revised within the constraints of its defined structure. When a DTD is produced, several distinct things are being specified:

(*a*)   the character set used, and the characters used for the various delimiters;

(*b*)   one or more sets of string-for-string replacements (used in some or all of the document);

(*c*)   the structures allowed in the document, and the code which identifies each element of the structure (thus, for example, a chapter, specified as being marked by a '<chp>' tag, must start with a title, which may not contain any markup, followed by one or more paragraphs or sub-headed sections); and

(*d*)   additional concurrent structures and/or correspondences between this structure and a structure defined in another DTD.

An SGML parser is a stripped-down compiler-compiler having the following functions:

- it takes (*a*) and generates a lexical analyser;

- it takes (*b*) and generates string replacement tables;

- it takes (*c*) and generates a syntax analyser (for any additional structure(s) specified in (*d*), it generates additional syntax analyser(s)); and then

- using (*b*), (*c*) and (*d*), and the additional functions programmed for that particular application, it generates a syntax-directed translator or other interface to another process. This is then used to check/transform the coded text and pass it in for processing as required.

4.3.1.2   The Development of SGML

The comprehensibility of the text was very important in the development of the SGML standard. It had to express accurately the abstract notions to be used in defining the document structures, yet be accessible to experts in technical writing and typography (rather than IT) who needed to be able to understand and criticise the kinds of structures allowed.

This was achieved to what was, in retrospect, a surprising degree by expressing the bare bones of the abstract structure of SGML in one of the simplest and most widely used notations available: BNF. BNF-like constructs are supplemented by a comprehensive explanatory glossary of the terms used in them, and a limited amount of accompanying text gives additional information which was difficult or impossible to express in the more formal notation. An extensive example was prepared early in the life of the standard, together with explanatory text covering the core concepts (but not all features). These were circulated (and updated) with the successive drafts of the standard, and finally published as Annexes to it. The accompanying text and examples occupy more pages than the standard itself. It is also very pertinent to the high quality of this standard that the editor implemented an SGML parser at the draft stage, which was modified and re-tested in parallel with subsequent changes.

The following is some sample text from the SGML standard:

10.1.6 External Identifier

[73]   external identifier = ("SYSTEM" |
       ("PUBLIC", *ps+*, *public identifier*)), (*ps+*, *system identifier*)?

[74]   public identifier = *minimum literal*

[75]   system identifier = (*lit*, *system data*, *lit*) | (*lita*, *system data*, *lita*)

The *system identifier* can be omitted if the system can generate it from the *public identifier* and/or other information available to it.

If "FORMAL YES" is specified on the *SGML declaration*, a *public identifier* is interpreted as a *formal public identifier* (see 10.2) and a formal public identifier error can occur.

NOTE — It is still a *minimum literal*, and all requirements pertaining to minimum literals apply.

10.1.6.1   Quantities

The length of a *system identifier*, exclusive of delimiters, cannot exceed the "LITLEN" quantity.

10.1.6.2   Capacities

The number of characters of *entity text* counted towards the ENTCHCAP capacity for an *external identifier* is that of its *system identifier* component, whether specified or generated (and exclusive of delimiters).

The following are two items from the corresponding 'Definitions':

4.239 public identifier: A minimum literal that identifies public text.

NOTES

1   The public identifiers in a document can optionally be interpretable as formal public identifiers.

2   The system is responsible for converting public identifiers to system identifiers.

4.313 system identifier: System data that specifies the file identifier, storage location, program invocation, data stream position, or other system-specific information that locates an external entity.

The corresponding explanation in Annex *B* is as follows:

B.6.2.3 External Entities

In many text processing systems, there are multiple classes of storage, such as files, library members, macro definitions, and symbols for text strings. Such system dependencies can be kept out of the body of the document by referencing external storage objects as entities:

    <!ENTITY part2 SYSTEM>

If the entity name is not sufficient to enable the system to identify the storage object, additional information (called the "system identifier") can be specified:

    <!ENTITY part2 SYSTEM "user.sectionX3.textfile">

The system identifier is delimited in the same manner as a parameter literal. The nature and syntax of the system identifier depends on a component of an SGML system called the *entity manager*, whose job it is to convert entity references into real system addresses.

B.6.2.4 Public Entities

An external entity that is known beyond the context of an individual document or system environment is called a "public entity". It is given a "public identifier" by an international, national or industry standard, or simply by a community of users who wish to share it.

One application of public entities would be shared document type definitions. Another would be shared "entity sets" of entity declarations that support the graphic symbols and terminology of specialized subject areas, such as mathematics or chemistry.

Public entities are declared in a manner similar to other external entities, except that a "public identifier specification" replaces the keyword "SYSTEM":

```
<!ENTITY    %   ISOgrk1
    PUBLIC "ISO 8879-1986//ENTITIES Greek Letters//EN">
```

The specification consists of the keyword "PUBLIC", the public identifier, which is delimited like a literal, and an optional system identifier (omitted in the example). The public identifier can contain only letters, digits, space, record ends and starts, and a few special characters; they are collectively known as the "minimum data" characters.

The main advantage of this approach was that it allowed members of the standards panel who were experts from publishing and technical writing backgrounds, but who were barely computer-literate, to achieve a sufficient working knowledge of the standard at draft stage to make valuable detailed comments. Without these the final standard would have been less widely applicable. The explanatory material published with the standard enabled quite a few people from publishing and technical writing backgrounds to start using it, or at least promoting it realistically to their management, in advance of the publication of an extensive secondary literature, and before fully documented implementations became available.

The main disadvantage was the poverty of the notation used, which caused many essential features of the abstract structures to be relegated to the text notes, or else left implicit (leading to differing interpretations). This applied particularly to semantic notions. Several substantive issues in this area are being resolved by consensus amongst those now implementing the standard. Some corrections have been published, but too much reliance still needs to be placed on the commonly accepted interpretation in reaching an exact understanding of some points. Hence someone working from the standard alone, in isolation from the community of users, could well come up with a significantly incompatible system.

4.3.1.3 Discussion

The SGML standard provides a good example of the use of formal notation in an application area where many end-users (and people on the standards bodies) are barely computer literate. The main lessons to be learnt from the SGML experience are:

- Where a standard needs input from potential users with limited IT backgrounds, this need should not be swept under the carpet, but be addressed by providing sufficient explanatory material and examples at the draft stage to enable them to comment on it properly. Straightforward formal notation is easier for such people to master (given adequate explanation) than English made unavoidably obscure by the development of an adequate verbal terminology and phraseology.

- Notations used should be the most simple, widely known and easy to learn which are suited to the purpose. Even when not wholly adequate, the value of using a widely known and accessible notation should carry great weight. Such a notation should, where possible, be known to the intended users of the standard, not just widely known in formal methods circles.

4.3.2   Office Document Architecture (ODA)

4.3.2.1   What is ODA?

ODA is a multi-part International Standard (ISO 8613). Its development was driven by the need for the open transfer of 'fixed' or 'revisable' office documents. (Open transfer refers to the fact that a creator and a recipient may have no agreements on, or understanding of, each other's computer system. The transfer mechanism is achieved by OSI and/or through the exchange of magnetic media.) ODA achieves this by standardising the semantics of the structural and content elements of documents.

The ODA architectural model is illustrated in Figure 6. It is an abstract structure composed of **objects**. According to the model, office documents are composed of two main groups of basic constituent objects: **logical objects** and **layout objects**. The constituents are combined in sets to produce structures which in turn describe more complex document characteristics. For example, the **Specific Layout Structure** has a set of constituents specifying how to format an instance of a document (such as pages containing frames). There are several structures in ODA:

- specific and **generic**;

- layout and **logical**; and

- supplementary **layout style sets** and **presentation style sets**.

The specific structure refers to an instance of a document; the generic to a class of documents. The logical structure groups the contents of a document according to its logical elements such as chapters, sections and paragraphs, whereas the layout structure, which is the result of the formatting process, groups document contents according to their physical appearance, such as pages, columns and blocks. Specific and generic are used to qualify layout and logical

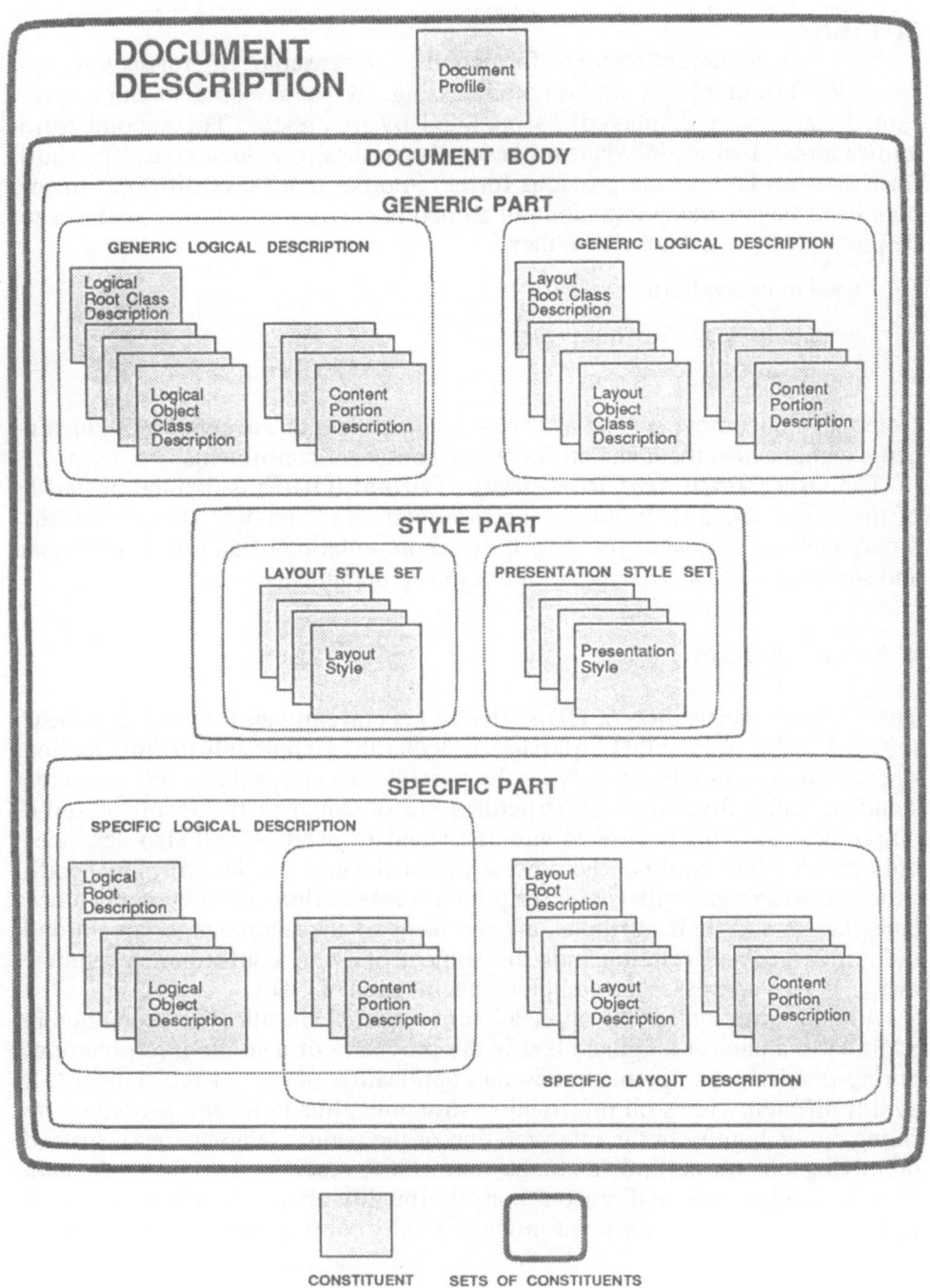

Figure 6. The ODA descriptive model of a document.

structures (such as **Generic Layout Structure** and **Specific Logical Structure**).

An ODA document may be 'formatted', 'processable' or 'formatted-processable'. The first form allows no processing, so that a document can be presented (printed or displayed) as intended by its creator. The second form allows a recipient to do whatever he or she wishes to a document. The third form satisfies both of the previous forms. In order that these different forms may be achieved, the composition of a document requires certain structures to be present. These **structures** either

- need to be explicitly present,

- need to be explicitly not present, or

- can be optionally present.

Note that a document is a set of constituents, structures are subsets of constituents within a document and attributes are subsets of constituents.

The **Office Document Interchange Format** (ODIF) is defined in Part 5 of the ODA standard. It defines a representation of the data stream (i.e. the binary coding format) of the descriptive representation of an ODA document and serves as a vehicle for the open transfer of documents.

4.3.2.2   FODA

The Formal Specification of ODA (FODA) is currently an ISO/IEC JTC1/SC 18/WG3 work item. FODA pursues a declarative approach to information structure description by specifying the possible structures that conform to the standard rather than how the structures are obtained as the result of some output process. This is aligned with the standard itself, which also describes only the structure, and not the processing, of documents. The formal specification is concerned with the descriptive representations of documents since constituents and their attributes are the basis of the interchange stream and their structure and relationships the subject of ODA conformance requirements. FODA addresses the complete specification of ODA.

A major criterion for the application of a formal specification technique in addition to a natural language text is the provision of a single interpretation, during the design, implementation and application phases of the standard. It avoids different views on information structures, functions and processes by ruling out ambiguity in the interpretation of the natural language text. Instead of relying on the natural language text alone, readers of FODA can gain clearer insights into, and reason more thoroughly about, the ODA standard. This enhances the probability of producing fully conformant implementations.

4.3.2.3   History and Development of FODA

The FODA work was initiated in 1985 at an ISO/WG3 meeting at the Hague, when it was decided then that a special working group (SWG) be formed whose purpose was to carry out a feasibility study on formalising ODA. The group considered many formal approaches and concluded that a formal specification of ODA was necessary for the future of the standard.

After showing examples of the techniques used in formalising ODA to a WG3 plenary, support was given by its members for the continuation of work on a draft formal specification of ISO 8613 Part 2.

The SWG produced a first draft of FODA which was undeveloped, although it did give a framework for the full formal specification of ISO 8613 Part 2, together with detailed terminology and notation. The formal work on ODA was subsequently endorsed by WG3 and a new version of the first draft of FODA was produced with an increased emphasis on readability.

A number of inconsistencies were identified in the English text version of the standard. These were addressed during a WG3 meeting in Austen in 1987. A second draft of FODA containing a full set of definitions was finally produced, which was circulated for comment at a Munich WG3 meeting. The SWG intends to complete the full formal specification of ODA by 1991. This will be published as Part 10 of the standard.

4.3.2.4   *Definition and Uses of FODA*

FODA is rigorous; it uses a formal methodology with foundations in mathematics and logic, hence it can be trusted to detect those parts of the standard that are incomplete, ill-defined or inconsistent. The formal methodology was developed by Durchholz and Richter and is known as **Information Modelling by Composition** (IMC). It uses an associated formal language, **IMCL** ('Information Modelling by Composition Language') [Ric88; App88b]. This technique extends IMC's mathematical and logic foundations by providing structures and operations especially suited to a complete and concise specification of the standard.

The formal basis of the notation is elementary *set theory* and *predicate logic*. It follows that most software technologists who have basic knowledge of the computing sciences should be able to understand the specification. Within the FODA documents the IMCL notation is accompanied by semi-formal English text clauses which, though not strictly part of the formal specification, do help the reader in understanding it (see Figure 7). Furthermore these clauses do provide an explicit link by referencing between the formal specification and those natural language clauses in the standard that are under definition. This gives some indirect confirmation about the completeness of the specification. FODA is structured so as to provide a high level of decomposition which aids the implementor by revealing just those parts of the standard under consideration at any one time.

The formal specification of ODA is expressed as a single formula in *first-order predicate calculus*. The formula consists of sub-formulae which are joined by the connective <u>*and*</u>:

$$\text{formula}_1 \; \underline{\textit{and}} \; \text{formula}_2 \; \underline{\textit{and}} \; ... \; \text{formula}_n$$

Semiformal Description 2.1

Predicate "is a document description" (2.3)

An entity *doc* is a document description if it is a collection of a single document profile *prof* (4) or if it is an entity which is processable, formatted processable or formatted (5–6), according to the value of the document profile attribute 'document architecture class' (7–13), with a 'resource-document' specified in the profile if any 'resource' is specified in the document (14–15).

Definition 2.1

```
1    ∀ doc
2    (₀ IsDocumentDescription(doc) iff
3       ∃ prof
4       (₁ IsDocumentProfilePart2²·¹(prof) and
5          (₂ doc = [prof] or IsProcessable²·⁴(doc) or
6             IsFormattedProcessable²·⁵(doc) or IsFormatted²·⁶(doc) ₂) and
7          doc ≠ [prof] impl
8          (₃ (₄ C ^ prof • 'document architecture class' = 'processable' iff
9             IsProcessable²·⁴(doc) ₄) and
10            (₅ C ^ prof • 'document architecture class' = 'formatted processable' iff
11            IsFormattedProcessable²·⁵(doc) ₅) and
12            (₆ C ^ prof • 'document architecture class' = 'formatted' iff
13            IsFormatted²·⁶(doc) ₆) and
14            ∀ cst ∈ doc
15            (₇ 'resource' ∈ NAMS¹·³¹(cst) impl 'resource-document' ∈ NAMS¹·³¹(prof) ₇) ₃) ₁) ₀)
```

Figure 7. An example definition within FODA.

These formulae are also called **definitions**. They define either concepts used in the natural English description of the standard, or subsidiary predicates and functions, which are introduced to enhance readability.

There are basic data types in addition to functions, the usual predicate logic quantification symbols and set operators. These are symbolic and numeric 'atoms', 'collections' (*sets*), 'nominations' (*sets of ordered pairs*) and 'catenations' (*lists or sequences*). Collections, nominations and catenations may contain any data structures as their elements, except that in nominations the name part of the pair (<name>:<value>) must be a symbolic atom.

A unique feature of IMCL is the concept of the **spot**, an abstract mechanism whose counterpart is the intuitive concept of **here**. In order to achieve this mechanism there exists a requirement to identify context. The spot allows a distinction to be drawn between a considered construct and its position within any composite construct which may comprise it in the IMCL universe.

FODA is specified according to purpose. It consists of **definitions** (*formulae*), some of which are concerned with ODA per se, such as **sets of constituents, constituents** and **attribute value ranges**, while others are concerned with the IMCL and its manipulation of the FODA constructs.

Testing conformance to the standard involves the development of test tools that determine whether a system can correctly transmit and/or receive conforming data streams. In the development of such tools, the formal specification will be important in order to ensure that the software is evaluating the system under test against the valid interpretation of the standard.

Figure 7 shows a simple definition in order to give a flavour of the formal description. Note, however, that this example does not necessarily reflect the final text of FODA.

The superscripts refer to the numbers of other definitions where the predicates and operators used within a definition are defined: thus the predicate **IsDocumentProfilePart2** is specified in Definition 2.1. The subscript numbers are used to pair opening brackets with their respective closing brackets. The numbers are not part of the syntax of FODA but are present to enhance readability. This is an appreciated aid in more complicated definitions and helps in development phases of FODA. For more detailed tutorials on the syntax and semantics of IMCL see [App88a; App88b; Kar88; Ric88].

FODA has already been used as a basis for the construction of a prototype conformance analyser. The analyser consists of FODA (IMCL) definitions and provides an executable version of the specification represented in Prolog. Prolog was particularly suitable as it is also based on the *predicate calculus*. In effect, the prototype conformance analyser implementation allows (through a one-to-one translation of FODA definitions) for an executable FODA.

A FODA-based **ODA Structure Analyser** (equivalent to the **ODA conformance analyser** but implemented in the C++ programming language to give more efficient processing than Prolog), analyses the structure of particular ODA documents. In addition, FODA-based **Content Architecture** (Raster, Geometric and Character) analysers can be added later and integrated in the **testing system** which will be used in the evaluation of ODA implementations. The development of test cases for conformance testing can also be based on FODA to form a system which can rigorously test all aspects of conformance to the ODA standard (i.e. data stream testing) and further by testing implementation features as well, as in the TODAC ('Testing ODA Conformance') Project. The formal specification can also be used as a basis for further development work (such as ODA **Extensions**) since it can provide an ideal model for accurately and economically predicting the effects of changes to the standard.

4.3.2.5   Developments in Formalising ODA

The formal work on ODA consists of the development of Part 10 of the standard (ISO 8613) with the following structure:

Title: Formal specifications
     Contents
     Foreword
     1   Scope
     2   Normative references
     3   Definitions
     4   Syntax and semantics of the specification language
     5   Structure of the formal specifications
     6   General functions, operators and predicates
     7   Formal specification of the document structures
     Annex A: Tutorial on the formal specification method
     Annex B: Formal specification of the document profile
     Annex C: Formal specification of the character content architectures
     Annex D: Formal specification of the raster content architectures
     Annex E: Formal specification of the geometric content architectures
     Annex F: Formal specification of the layout process

Thus formal specifications of the document profile (Part 4) and the character, raster and geometric content architectures (Parts 6, 7 and 8) will be added to the text of Part 10 as Normative Annexes. In addition there is an Informative Annex containing a tutorial on the formal specification method. A FODA version of the ODA document **Layout Process** (which is an Informative Annex to Part 2) will also be provided in a Normative Annex to Part 10: this part of FODA is exceptional in that it actually specifies something which is not precisely specified in the standard itself.

4.3.2.6   Conclusions

There exists at present a need for a formal specification technique with a rigorous mathematical basis to describe information structures when creating standards for document processing systems. Owing to its lack of precision, ambiguities and even inconsistencies can be permanent features of a natural language specification, much to the chagrin of authors and readers alike. Even though a natural English text may still be the final form of a standard, it is worthwhile making the effort to specify it formally. This will improve a standard and provide a definitive reference document to answer all the questions arising from attempted interpretations of the English text versions. In addition to creating a rigorous foundation for a standard, a formal specification can be used in the development of standards test tools, such as the forthcoming ODA Structure Analyser to be derived from FODA.

4.4 Graphics

4.4.1 Introduction

This section reviews work in the application of FDTs for software specification to standards for computer graphics. We start with a brief overview of graphics standards and conclude with some thoughts on the state of the art and future directions.

The motivation for the use of formal description techniques in graphics standards stems from three sources:

- Graphics standards as presently under development in ISO are specifications of products. As such they need to be defined concisely and unambiguously. The need for precision argues for the use of mathematics.

- Graphics standards are becoming increasingly complex, yet there are (or certainly should be) components and mechanisms that are common across a range of standards. The management of complexity and reusability of definitions is becoming an issue in standards development; mathematics can provide a handle onto this. Structure and reasoning about structures are topics which are covered very well in Milner's lucid paper [Mil86].

- As software systems are used in an increasing number of what may be described as safety critical systems [Lev86], the questions of whether a specification is formally correct and whether the software system satisfies the specification assume a special significance. The area of computer graphics does not escape from this. Before the question of conformance to a specification can be formally addressed, one must have a formal definition of the specification in question.

4.4.2 Standards for Computer Graphics

Standardisation activities have existed in computer graphics since the early 1970s and a family of standards for computer graphics is now emerging from ISO/IEC. This family of standards covers a broad range of graphics requirements from application program interfaces for the generation and interactive manipulation of 3D graphics to device-level interfaces for the transfer of graphical information.

The major standards in progress are:

- **GKS** (Graphical Kernel System)—a set of basic functions for 2D device-independent computer graphics programming (ISO 7942);

- **CGM** (Computer graphics metafile for transfer and storage of picture description information)—a device-independent data exchange format for computer graphics pictures (ISO 8632);

- **CGI** (Interface techniques for dialogues with graphical devices)—a set of basic elements for the control and data exchange between device-independent and device-dependent levels in graphics (ISO 9636);

- **GKS-3D** (Graphical Kernel System for 3 Dimensions)—an extension of GKS to provide the basic functions for computer graphics programming in 3D (ISO 8805);

- **PHIGS** (Programmer's Hierarchical Interactive Graphics System)—a set of functions for computer graphics programming in environments requiring rapid modification of graphical data that describes geometrically related objects (ISO 9592);

- **Language bindings**—bindings of the functions and data types of the functional standards to standardised programming languages (ISO 8651; ISO 8806; ISO 9637; ISO 9593);

- **Registration**—a registration mechanism is being set up to deal with the standardisation of primitive aspects, generalised primitives, escape functions and other graphical entities;

- **Conformance testing of implementations of graphics standards**—the purpose of this project is twofold: first to specify the characteristics of standardised test sets for use in determining the conformance of implementations of graphics standards and secondly to provide direction to developers of functional standards concerning conformance rules; and

- **Reference model**—this project is developing a basic reference model for computer graphics standards.

GKS, GKS FORTRAN and Pascal language bindings and CGM have been published as International Standards. Final text has been agreed for the GKS Ada language binding, GKS-3D and PHIGS and Procedures for the Registration of Graphical Items. The first five-year review of GKS is under way.

Since most of the applications of formal methods to graphics concern GKS, it is appropriate to give a short description of GKS here.

GKS is a two-dimensional graphics system which aims to provide an interface between applications programs and a wide variety of graphics devices. It caters for both graphical output and graphical input. GKS defines six **output primitives**:

- **Polyline**, which draws a sequence of connected line segments;

- **Polymarker**, which marks a sequence of points with the same symbol;

- **Fill area**, which displays a specified area;

- **Text**, which draws a string of characters;

- **Cell array**, which displays an image composed of cells with specified colours or grey scales; and

- **Generalised drawing primitive** (GDP), a controlled method of adding more exotic primitives, for example, conic arcs and splines.

The concept of a **workstation** in GKS is an abstraction from a physical device which maps physical output primitives to abstract output primitives and physical input primitives to abstract input primitives. It represents zero or one display surfaces and zero or more input devices as a configuration of abstract devices. An application program may direct output to more than one workstation simultaneously.

GKS divides the output pipeline of graphics into two parts. The application program specifies co-ordinate data in an output primitive in **world co-ordinates** (WC). The first part of the pipeline transforms world co-ordinates into a virtual device space called **normalised device co-ordinates** (NDC). The second part transforms NDC to the **device co-ordinates** (DC) of the display surface. This second transformation allows individual workstations to view different areas of NDC space.

The appearance of primitives on the display surface (for example colour, line width, fill area interior style), is controlled by their **aspects**. GKS provides two mechanisms for this—individual specification and bundled specification. In the former, values of the aspects are specified directly and are associated with primitives as they are created. A workstation which does not support a particular aspect value requested, has to match the value as closely as possible. In bundled specification, a level of indirection is introduced. In the virtual NDC space, primitives have values associated with them. Workstations can specify the aspect values associated with each index, allowing output with different index values to be differentiated across a wide range of devices with differing capabilities.

GKS has a segment storage scheme which provides a single level of storage structure for saving and manipulating picture parts. Segments have some attributes which affect their characteristics, for example visibility and highlighting.

GKS has a well-defined input model. GKS defines a set of logical input devices (LOCATOR, VALUATOR, PICK, CHOICE, STRING and STROKE) which can be used in three operating modes: REQUEST, SAMPLE and EVENT. The application program can control various attributes of input devices such as prompt/echo type and the region of the display surface in which echoing will occur.

4.4.3 Applications of Formal Specification to Computer Graphics

4.4.3.1 Early Work

One of the earliest papers in this area is Guttag and Horning's [Gut80] which describes the specification of a high-level interface to a display. Their approach combines algebraic specification with pre and post conditions. Systems are viewed as a state and a set of mechanisms (called **routines**) for changing and extracting information from that state. Actions of the 'outside world' are also modelled as routines, so that the current state of a system is always the result of routines previously performed. States are defined algebraically by (i) a set of function names that can be used to refer to system states, (ii) a set of questions that can be asked about these states and (iii) a set of equations designed to imply answers to the questions one can pose about states. The information contained in each state is thus defined indirectly in terms of replies to questions that may be asked about it.

Their paper discusses the design of a display interface. The user can simultaneously display several disjoint blocks of displayable information called **pictures**. A **view** is a spatial arrangement of pictures, which may overlap. The contents of a picture is a number (possibly zero) of components. Components are either text, figures or views. The idea is similar to windows and sub-windows in a window management system [Hop86a].

The paper presents a specification for the display system and then shows how it is possible to pose and answer questions about the design from the formal specification. For example, it is shown that pictures are not transparent or translucent (i.e. if two pictures overlap, the bottom one has no effect on what one sees through the top one). This paper made an important contribution by showing how specification can be used for formal analysis and reasoning about a design.

Sorensen [Sor81] subsequently presented the design of a similar display interface in an early version of the Z specification language which showed the power of this language in structuring a fairly complex specification. The capabilities of Z in this direction have been much improved since that paper was written.

Mallgren's paper [Mal82] on the formal specification of graphic data types is an important contribution. He identifies four general concepts which he uses as the basis for the specification of graphics data types, **region, picture, graphic transformation** and **hierarchical picture structure**. Each concept is treated as a collection of objects operated upon by well-defined operations. For example, the key operation on a hierarchical picture structure is **display**, which converts it into the resultant picture.

Mallgren then incorporates these concepts into abstract data types. His primary motivation for doing this is to provide a framework for the concepts needed in graphics programming languages. In the traditional approach graphic objects have been represented in the standard (general) data types provided by programming languages (e.g. **integer, real** and the two constructors **record** and **array**). The argument against this approach is that the graphics programmer has to work with abstractions that do not correspond to those used in graphics and in consequence has to be aware of representations at an inappropriate level of detail. Also responsibility for the integrity of the structures constructed rests with the programmer.

To specify graphics operations a combination of algebraic and operational approaches is used. Operations on regions are specified in terms of equivalent operations on sets of points.

Mallgren's paper then goes on to describe a simple graphics programming language and shows how it is possible to reason about programs in this language. Mallgren's PhD dissertation [Mal83] discusses the application of this technique to the specification of a part of the GSPC Core graphics system [GSP79] and describes a technique for the specification of interaction.

4.4.3.2 Specification of Standards for Computer Graphics

The German DIN group produced the first designs for the **Graphical Kernel System** (GKS), which after a lengthy international review became the first ISO standard for computer graphics programming (ISO 7942) [Hop86b]. In both the USA and Germany there was interest in how to give formal definitions of such systems. An early example is the paper by Eckert [Eck80] which explored the use of Parnas' trace technique as a basis for a GKS specification.

Formal approaches to the definition of graphics standards were considered at length in a series of workshops funded by the EEC on the Certification of Graphics Software [Duc82; Bro82] in 1981/82. An *ad hoc* sub-committee of the ANSI committee responsible for graphics (X3H3) also considered the problems of formally defining graphics systems. They examined a number of specification techniques which have been applied to programming languages, but concluded that none was adequate for specifying graphics systems [Car83a; Car83b]. Rosenthal [Ros80] proposed the use of Pascal as a specification language, effectively by defining a reference implementation. This approach has many merits but suffers from the drawbacks that it is difficult to reason at that (low) level of abstraction, it unavoidably overspecifies how graphics primitives are to be processed and it requires the use of a particular language binding (functional graphics standards are defined independently of programming languages).

In parallel with the international development of GKS, the ANSI graphics group worked on a proposal for a minimal graphics system known as the **Programmer's Minimal Interface for Graphics** (PMIG) [ANS82]. Although this system never became an ANSI standard (in fact the functionality of PMIG is contained in one level of the ANSI GKS standard), PMIG is important because Carson and Post gave a formal definition [Car83a; Car83b].

The difficult part of any attempt to specify graphics systems is how to treat the rendering of primitives on a display. The difficulty is how to accommodate the range of physical display hardware in an abstract representation whilst being able to say something about how primitives should appear on the display surface. Some authors [Mar85b] have looked at the problem of specifying how primitives should appear when displayed. The difficulty here tends to be that these approaches are specific to a particular device class, for example raster displays. The approach taken by Carson is to model the output of a graphics system as abstract data types, and regard the display process as a binding of these abstract data types to a physical display device. This has the merit that the functionality of a graphics system can be specified, implemented and even certified without producing a single picture. The description of what a line should look like is regarded as a binding issue and not a specification issue.

Gnatz [Gna83] describes a framework for the specification of graphics systems based on an algebraic approach, the CIP wide spectrum language of the Munich CIP project. The key idea here is that of transforming a specification by a series of correctness-preserving transformations into an implementation.

Gnatz goes on to discuss the specification of graphics metafiles for the transfer and storage of graphical information. His technique is an elegant one which uses the mathematical notion of 'lifting' to model delayed evaluation.

The idea is that the metafile corresponds to a sequence of graphical functions to which arguments are bound, but which have not been evaluated. The action of metafile interpretation is then modelled as evaluation and Gnatz is able to prove that two sequences of procedure calls are equivalent, the one generating graphical output directly, the other via intermediate generation and interpretation of a metafile. This paper, along with that by Richter [Ric86] make the important point that considerations of syntax alone are not sufficient to define a graphics metafile. Semantics of the primitives also need to be given to ensure that when a primitive is stored in a metafile and subsequently interpreted, the original primitive is obtained. Generation and interpretation of metafiles are in this sense inverse operations.

4.4.3.3 Applications to GKS

The application of formal specification techniques to the Graphical Kernel System (GKS) and other emerging graphics standards has resulted in a number of papers.

[Duc88] examines the GKS concept of implicit regeneration. A small subset of GKS is specified in the VDM notation and a proof is given that, under defined circumstances, the same picture is obtained regardless of whether a change is made by dynamic modification or implicit regeneration. The specification in this paper is developed in a number of stages and in more detail in [Duc86a].

[Duc87a] compares VDM with a property-oriented method, OBJ [Gog82; Col84; Fut85]. An example specification, roughly that in [Duc86a] is described in both techniques and comparisons are drawn. One of the main benefits of OBJ lies in the modularity constructs it provides, which enable the structure of the problem to be expressed more clearly.

The work described so far has concentrated on what may be described as the control structures in GKS. [Duc86b] gives definitions of the five main output primitives in GKS—polyline, polymarker, text, fill area and cell array. Primitives are described at three levels, corresponding to world co-ordinates (WC), normalized device co-ordinates (NDC), and device co-ordinates (DC). [Ond87] also looks at the problem of describing graphical primitives and follows a somewhat similar approach.

[Arn87] is a first attempt to combine the ideas contained in previous papers by Duce and his collaborators. The motivation for this paper comes from the work of Arnold and Reynolds on configurable models of graphics systems [Rey86]. This paper concentrates on a single output primitive, polyline, but should provide a general framework for a GKS specification.

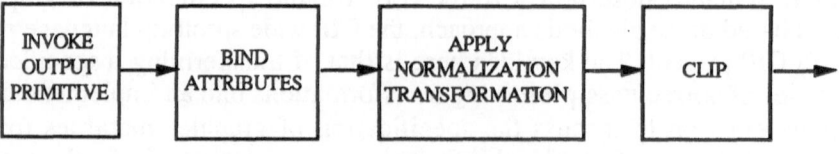

Figure 8. An example of a graphics pipeline.

The paper is based on the idea of a graphics pipeline, in which respect it resembles the PMIG specification of Carson and Post, but the approach to the specification is different. An example of a graphics pipeline is shown in Figure 8. Processes in the pipeline act on primitives and generate primitives. The approach taken is based on the observation that not all the information associated with a primitive is known at every stage of the pipeline. Effectively the pipeline processes add to, subtract from, or otherwise modify the information contained in the primitive entering process. Pipeline processes also have an associated state that can be set by GKS functions.

The effect of a pipeline is obtained by combining the effects of the operations in the pipeline in such a way that the output from one operation is identified with the input to the next. Z contains an operation combinator called **piping** for this purpose. Each pipeline process has an associated state and operations which modify this state can be readily written.

The benefits of this approach over those explored earlier is that the global system state can be partitioned between processes. This means that the descriptions of individual processes become simpler, because only the parts of the state that concern each process need to be considered. It also provides a mechanism for future expansion, in that new processes can be easily added to the pipeline with their associated states. It is thought (though this has not yet been confirmed) that this framework is extensible to GKS-3D.

It must be emphasized that the **processes** in this model are not concurrent. However recent theoretical work in combining the Z and CSP notations should make it possible to describe pipelines whose components are processes in the usual meaning of the word.

The insights gained by Duce and collaborators from attempting to formally specify the output side of GKS are summarised in a paper for the Eurographics GKS Review Workshop [Duc87c]. For example, attempts to specify the GKS output primitives show that the fill area primitive is inadequate for describing primitives containing holes, and that the GKS definition of cell array is ambiguous with regard to the colour of pixels on the boundary of adjacent cells of different colours in certain cases. These may seem very minor points, but many of the comments submitted in the PHIGS DIS ballot were from implementors of PHIGS who were raising issues at just this level of detail. It is also interesting to note that typically these comments could be addressed very easily in a formal specification, but trying to find unambiguous English expressions of the behaviour required was very difficult.

Some work has been done in connection with the development of GKS-3D and PHIGS to show how, by making some extensions to GKS, it would be possible to describe the generation of graphical output by PHIGS in terms of GKS [Duc86c]. Essentially this involved adding an extra attribute to the GKS primitives and providing an alternative mechanism for controlling visibility, highlighting and detectability. Specifications were given in OBJ and it was shown how the systems could work together. [Duc89a] takes this idea further. Such an approach could have greatly simplified the description of PHIGS and provided a useful form of compatibility between the standards. However these ideas were rejected by the ISO Working Group at that time.

The input side of GKS has received less attention. [Duc87b] examines the data structures in the GKS input model and proposes some alternative ways to realize the GKS functionality which provide a cleaner overall structure and readily permit the kinds of extensions which GKS users frequently demand, for example the ability to group input devices together to form composite devices, to construct compound input values from devices of different types controlled by the same trigger or set of triggers. These ideas are now being considered by the GKS Review. [Duc89b] uses CSP to give a specification of the GKS input model as a set of co-operating processes.

[Rug87a] look at the data structures in GKS from a VDM standpoint and have produced a thorough report on their findings. Again, looking at GKS from a formal specification standpoint led to proposals which would produce a simpler and more elegant document.

4.4.4   Future Developments

There is still much work to be done to demonstrate the benefits of formal specification, but the work done so far has convinced a small number of authors of the promise of formal methods as a descriptive notation for the communication of designs and as a notation for investigating the properties of designs. To convince the wider graphics standards-making community of the value of formal description, there is a need for more case studies, more education and demonstrations in real projects that using formal techniques leads to a better quality product.

4.5   Open Systems Interconnection

4.5.1   Formal Methods in Computer Communication Standards

4.5.1.1   Introduction

In recent years much effort in the International Standards arena has been devoted to the progression of specifications for protocols designed to bring about open data communications, in which the problems can be overcome of connecting to one another the systems of different vendors. Within the context of the OSI seven-layer model protocols have been designed to provide different levels of communications service. Although some difficulties of interpretation remain, the majority of these standards have reached the status of full international standards and are being adopted by major manufacturers.

Computer communication systems present tough problems to the software engineer. Concurrency and non-determinism make most development tasks much more difficult than for other kinds of system. Despite the use of various systematic development techniques, there is still no agreed and systematic discipline of engineering in this field. Over the years, however, experience and research have steadily built a corpus of insight into the major technical problems and there is now a firm foundation for the introduction of formal methods.

4.5.1.2 Historical Background

The convergence of computing and telecommunications began with the introduction of remote batch terminals in the 1960s. Programmed drivers for these devices were among the first examples of communication software. A typical device driver would involve various handshaking sequences in which fairly simple items of data were exchanged. This characteristic led naturally to the use of finite-state modelling in the development of driver software.

Finite state machine theory lay fortuitously in the common ground between switching theory and automata theory and was known to both telecommunications and software specialists. For some years it provided a useful means for the specification, design, verification, implementation and testing of communication software. By the late 1970s, however, the microprocessor had made it physically and economically feasible to produce very complex computer networks. For systems of this scale finite-state techniques soon became intractably difficult and more powerful alternatives were badly needed.

Fortunately, just at that time, theoretical research began to produce new methods for dealing with communicating systems. Milner's *Calculus of Communicating Systems* [Mil80] was a landmark in this field. Hoare was also developing related ideas [Hoa85a]. The field of study now known as **process algebra** came into being and brought more manageable techniques to the attention first of the academic community and then of practising system engineers. Process algebra was to provide the basis for one of the first standardised formal specification techniques. Currently such techniques are being used in the field of international standards for open systems interconnection and have also been usefully applied in system development.

4.5.1.3 The Current Situation

The use of formal and semi-formal description techniques for the specification of ISO Open System Interconnection standards and CCITT international telecommunications standards is well advanced. Five specification techniques of greater or lesser formality are currently used in computer communication standards: LOTOS, Estelle, SDL, ASN.1 and TTCN. These are described in Section 3.2.2 above.

4.5.1.4 An Example: Multiplexing

The following extract is taken from a current ISO draft technical report offering guidelines on the application of Estelle, LOTOS and SDL (ISO 10167). It shows a simple definition, that of a multiplexing function, expressed using each of the three methods, and is intended to give a general flavour of the resulting specification in each case. Note that this extract does not necessarily reflect the final text of the technical report.

Multiplexing

The example used is a Multiplexing/Demultiplexing Function which multiplexes data from one Service onto an underlying Service.

Estelle Representation

In Estelle, Multiplexing applies to interactions of two or more Users who request a Service (by Service Primitives) at two or more interaction points. These interactions are mapped by a Protocol Entity onto one underlying interaction point of the underlying Service Provider.

In the simplest case, multiplexing data from several Users onto a single underlying Service is accomplished by adding User identification to User interactions, and then sending the result via the underlying Service. Demultiplexing works in the opposite direction by removing User identification, and then sending the remaining information to that user.

The following example assumes that the necessary channels, types, variables etc. have been defined. This Estelle fragment gives two transitions, one to multiplex from any of *NUsers* Users onto the underlying Server, and the other to demultiplex from the Server onto the Users.

```
trans {multiplex}
  any id : i .. NUsers do
    when User[id].UDataReq(UserData)
      begin
         output Server.SDataReq(id, UserData)
      end;

trans {demultiplex}
  when Server.SDataInd(id, UserData)
    begin
       output User[id].UDataInd(UserData)
    end;
```

LOTOS Representation

A simple multiplexer/demultiplexer accepts data from different sources, distinguished by their identifier, and forwards it with a tag indicating its source. For example:

```
process MuxDemux
  [U,L] (USap:USapSort,LSap:LSapSort) : noexit :=

    Mux [U,L] (USap,LSap)
|||
    Demux [U,L] (USap,LSap)

  where

  process Mux
    [U,L] (USap:USapSort,LSap:LSapSort) : noexit :=

    choice UEp:UEpSort, Ud:OctetString []
      (
         U ! USap ! UEp ! UDataReq(Ud);
         L ! LSap ! LDataReq(UEp,Ud);
         Mux [U,L] (USap,LSap)
      )

  endproc (* Mux *)
```

```
    process Demux
      [U,L] (USap:USapSort,LSap:LSapSort) : noexit :=

      choice UEp:UEpSort, Ud:OctetString []
        (
          L ! LSap ! LDataInd(UEp,Ud);
          U ! USap ! UEp ! UDataInd(Ud);
          Demux [U,L] (USap,LSap)
        )

    endproc (* Demux *)

  endproc (* MuxDemux *)
```

where

- *U* and *L* are the gates for communication at the Upper and Lower Services;

- *USap* refers to the Upper Service Access Point identifier, and *LSap* refers to the Lower Service Access Point identifier;

- *UEp* refers to the Upper Service Endpoint identifier; and

- *OctetString* is the standard library sort, used for Service Data Units.

SDL Representation

Multiplexing can be handled in SDL by mapping Protocol Data Units from different Associations onto a single Association (channel and receiver identity), tagging each PDU with a final destination identifier.

```
    PROCESS Multiplexing;
      ...
      INPUT PDU(Par1,Par2,Par3);
      OUTPUT MediumPDU(Par1,Par2,Par3,RefNo);

    PROCESS Demultiplexing;
      ...
      INPUT MediumPDU(Par1,Par2,Par3,RefNo);
      DECISION (RefNo);
        (PathA):OUTPUT PDU(Par1,Par2,Par3) VIA PATHA;
        ...
        (PathN):OUTPUT PDU(Par1,Par2,Par3) VIA PATHN;
      ENDDECISION
```

4.5.1.5   Limitations and Prospects

At present none of the five techniques is fully satisfactory. The main problem areas are expressive capacity, life-cycle coverage, and the receptiveness of the industry. A comparison of Estelle and LOTOS is instructive.

LOTOS is currently the only standardised description technique with fully formal semantics. It has been used very successfully to produce formal specifications of several OSI protocols and services.

Estelle is primarily a language for design and implementation, although it does support some forms of analysis which are essentially forms of requirement verification. Experience of use in both Europe and North America has shown, however, that Estelle texts are often verbose and overspecific. This is perhaps a predictable consequence of being based on a programming language.

Estelle can describe timing in systems. LOTOS has no concept of time although it could easily be added. Estelle has concrete data types and can be compiled. LOTOS has abstract data types which can only be interpreted. LOTOS can be used effectively for both functional and design specification but has not been used for implementation. Estelle is inappropriate for functional specification, inflexible for design specification but eminently implementable.

The characteristics of Estelle and LOTOS have strongly influenced the attitudes of industry towards them. At first sight Estelle seems more familiar than LOTOS and has gained support because of its implementability. Several Estelle users have, however, become disillusioned by its cumbrousness and have turned to LOTOS only to be disappointed for want of a mature implementation route.

From the user's point of view there is no fully satisfactory formal description technique for communication systems. However, developers of formal methods, though mainly academics, nowadays often have industrial research partners. Academic research has outgrown 'toy' examples and now attacks problems on a realistic industrial scale. Academics are having to come to terms with quality assurance and to stop dismissing serious engineering as implementation details. They must devise new techniques with better focused expressive power which can also support substantially automated progression from functional specification to implementation. This goal should be reachable by the end of the century.

4.5.2   OSI Protocol Conformance Testing

As a natural progression from the relative stability of the standards the need has been recognised for a standard way of testing communications products which claim to implement the OSI protocols. In parallel with the later phase of the standardisation process, work has begun with the aim of defining methods for deriving suitable tests and for the specification of these tests (ISO 9646). ISO have provided guidelines to assist those involved in the derivation of tests for OSI protocols. The overall goal is to have associated with each protocol a set of standard tests which a product must pass if it is to be able to claim conformance.

4.5.2.1   The ISO Method of Conformance Test (Derivation and) Specification

It has been recognised that it will not always be possible to test all OSI products in the same way: observation of protocol behaviour may be restricted by the chosen implementation method, something which the standards do not specify. For this reason ISO have defined a variety of test methods, each of which formalises an architecture involving the product under test and a testing system (ISO 9646).

In the ISO method of test derivation the process begins with a set of English-language test purposes organised in a structure which reflects the aspects of the given protocol to be tested. Once the test purposes have been agreed, work then moves to the specification of the behaviour involved, that is the dynamic interactions between test system and implementation under test. Given that some OSI protocols may be tested using more than one of the standard test methods, it is necessary to specify behaviour independently of test method. Such specifications are known as Generic Test specifications. For each test method the Generic Tests are then used to specify the behaviour specific to the methods. These specifications are known as Abstract Test specifications. The language used for both types of test specification is the Tree and Tabular Combined Notation (TTCN).

4.5.2.2   Tree and Tabular Combined Notation (TTCN)

The definition of TTCN appears in Part 3 of the International Standard relating to Conformance Testing Methodology and Framework (ISO 9646) and has been progressed by the ISO Working Group JTC1/SC21/WG1.

TTCN is a notation which provides a complete set of mechanisms for the definition of a set of protocol conformance tests (a 'test suite'). Briefly, the components of a TTCN test suite are as follows.

- **Suite Overview.** This section contains a general introduction with information needed for the presentation and understanding of the test suite.

- **Declarations Part.** This section contains descriptions of the components which comprise the suite. These are typically objects used in the behavioural model such as the **Protocol Data Units** (PDUs) exchanged by the test system and the implementation under test, any timers used in the protocol and the points in the architecture at which the implementation can be controlled and observed (**Points of Control and Observation**—PCOs). Also defined here are any abbreviations used in the suite.

- **Dynamic Part.** This part comprises three sections containing tables specifying test behaviour in terms of event occurrences at the declared PCOs:

  - behaviour description for each test ;

  - a library of test step dynamic behaviour descriptions; and

  - a library of default dynamic behaviour descriptions.

- **Constraints Part.** This part contains specified instances of objects used in the dynamic part. Generally these are descriptions of PDUs which have specific values.

In the specification of individual tests all behaviour is described in terms of events observable within a part of the test system. In a simple test, the test system might send some data to the implementation and then wait to receive a response. The behaviour description specifies this interaction and provides cross-references to the constraints part of the suite where the exact data values are defined. In each test the TTCN specification assigns a verdict to the test on the basis of the observed behaviour of the implementation. This verdict may be one of PASS, FAIL or INCONC (inconclusive). The verdict PASS is given if the behaviour of the implementation is fully conformant, the verdict FAIL if the implementation violates the protocol conformance requirements and the verdict INCONC if the implementation exhibits behaviour which provides no indication as to its conformance within the context of the specific purposes of the test.

4.5.2.3 *Conformance Testing of FTAM in the CTS-WAN Project*

CTS-WAN (Conformance Testing Services over Wide Area Networks) is a CEC-sponsored project with the goal of establishing harmonised conformance testing services for OSI protocols throughout the member states of the European Community. Work began in mid-1986 and is due to be completed before mid-1989. The contractors in the project are required to submit to ISO any work done on the specification of protocol tests. All tests used in the project must therefore be specified in TTCN. In CTS-WAN different test systems are being used in different countries: in order to ensure harmonisation contractors must perform equivalence demonstrations to show that (the execution of) tests implemented on one test system produce the same results as those given by the same tests executed on a different system.

Part of the CTS-WAN project is designated to the development of conformance test services for the ISO protocol File Transfer, Access and Management (FTAM) (ISO 8571). The project is working with the subset of the protocol defined by the functional profile which is now a European standard (ENV 41-204). The subset involved allows the transfer of unstructured files together with management of the remote filestore.

The specification of tests in TTCN attempts to limit the problem of ambiguity of interpretation leading to different test implementation. This is particularly important in testing since the situation is clearly unacceptable in which testing with one test system shows an implementation's conformance but testing with another shows areas of non-conformance. The truly international nature of data communications emphasises this point: an implementation cannot be viewed as conformant within the frontiers of one nation, and perhaps therefore have permission to use the network, while it is non-conformant in another country and therefore denied network access.

The CTS-WAN project shows clearly the advantages of using some formal method for specification. By definition a specification is independent of the implementation choice. In CTS-WAN FTAM two test systems are being used, each of which employs a radically different way of realising the implementation of the specified tests. In this case, where equivalence of execution results is paramount, the TTCN test specification is used as the reference document by which to assess the correctness of test implementation. Furthermore, the TTCN document will be available to any organisation which chooses to submit an implementation to CTS-WAN conformance testing. The specification is therefore required to be an unambiguous statement of what takes place in each test execution, including—perhaps most important for the product implementor—the exact circumstances under which an implementation is declared conformant or non-conformant.

FTAM is a protocol of the OSI Application Layer (Layer 7). FTAM uses the services of the ACSE protocol, also resident in the Application Layer but used only to establish and terminate connections to a remote system, and those of the Presentation Layer (Layer 6). Beneath the Presentation Layer is the Session Layer whose protocol is used to control dialogue synchronisation and to transfer the data specific to the protocols in the layers above. Within the CTS-WAN FTAM Project implicit testing of the ACSE and Presentation protocols is required: the PCO used in tests is therefore the interface between the Session and Presentation Layers in the test system. This places the requirement on test specifications to define the behaviour in three protocols—Presentation, ACSE and FTAM. For test purposes, however, behaviour is examined in the FTAM protocol only. The facility provided in TTCN for abbreviations has been found to be useful to solve this problem. A set of abbreviations, similar to macros, has been defined which shows the events in the Presentation and ACSE protocols associated with an event in the FTAM protocol. Abbreviations are given names which have meaning in terms of FTAM only. Tests can therefore be specified as occurrences of FTAM protocol events, while the lower layer behaviour is available in macro expansions. In this special situation the occurrence of an unexpected event in a protocol other than FTAM always leads to the assignment of the INCONC (inconclusive) verdict (see above).

In the OSI protocols of the Presentation and Application Layers the data structures exchanged in communication (PDUs) are specified in ASN.1 (ISO 8824). Before being passed to the Session Layer for transfer these structures are encoded into a byte stream using the ASN.1 Basic Encoding Rules (ISO 8825). On receipt of data from the Session Layer the reverse decode function must be applied to transform the byte stream into an ASN.1 object. In these protocols the numbers of events and states are relatively small whereas the ASN.1 PDUs are large and complex structures. The manipulations of, and modifications to, these structures required to be performed by a test system are difficult to specify. TTCN provides a facility for users to define operators specific to a test suite: this has been found to be especially useful in the CTS-WAN FTAM test suite.

The complexity of the PDUs has led to a large part on constraints in the test suite specification. For the handling of ASN.1-defined PDUs TTCN provides the ASN.1 modular method for constraint construction. Using this method the writer specifies a base PDU containing all possible parameters each with a fixed value; from this base many variations may be created by performing single parameter substitutions or omissions. This technique has been used to good effect in the CTS-WAN work.

4.5.2.4 Conclusion

Until relatively recently TTCN has been a (conformance test) specification
language without a clear definition. It had therefore appeared in many different dialects and been viewed as an informal notation. Its use for test specification within the ISO arena and in such projects as CTS-WAN has hastened its
progression to a state in which it is clear, well-understood and above all, useful
for the production of unambiguous protocol conformance test specifications.

The NCC is a contractor in the CTS-WAN FTAM Project and responsible
for the production of TTCN specifications for File Transfer related tests. The
tests have been available in the public domain since April 1989.

5.
Current Practice:
Issues and Guidelines

5.1 Introduction

Standards are perceived as important for industry at large, and for software development in particular. They were singled out for special mention in a recent report by the Cabinet Office's **Advisory Committee for Applied Research and Development** (ACARD) [ACA86]. Yet they come in for much criticism. All too frequently, they fail to do the job that they were intended for. The same is, of course, true of software itself, and in this area the ACARD report also had some strong recommendations, foremost amongst which were the exploitation of software components and the use of formal methods. Could formal methods also have a similar role to play in the development and use of standards?

ISO has recently been actively considering the exploitation of formal methods and is beginning to publish policy statements in this area. An important such statement is provided by the recommendations of the ISO/IEC JTC1 (formerly ISO/TC97) Special Working Group on Formal Description Techniques contained in a report entitled 'Criteria for the use and applicability of formal description techniques' [ISO87]. This report contains a generally helpful set of criteria for the use and applicability of FDTs in the development of standards.

In this section we attempt to identify some of the main issues that arise in the development and expression of standards, emphasizing in each case some positive and negative aspects of using formal methods and providing some general guidelines as appropriate.

5.2 Quality and Correctness

The main potential benefit of using formal methods in the development and expression of a standard is to improve the quality of the product. This must be the general aim of anyone seriously considering the use of formal methods at some stage within the 'standards development process'. We have already discussed in some detail the meaning of 'quality' in the context of standards (see Section 2).

Formal methods can clearly have a beneficial role throughout the standards development process. In the early stages, for example, they can bring about considerable clarification during the development and expression of the underlying conceptual model for a standard or set of standards. They can also define precisely the relation between the components of a standard and between the components of different standards. This aids integration by allowing a collection of standards to be formulated in a compatible notation, and the formal properties of the collection (such as mutual consistency) to be assessed as a whole. In short, suitable formal methods could provide an excellent basis for project planning of the standards development within ISO.

Later in the development process, formal methods can improve the quality of a standard during its use by enabling it to be expressed clearly, unambiguously and concisely in a way that natural language, however carefully restricted, does not allow (the contribution of FODA to the ODA standard demonstrates this). A side benefit is to reduce the dependency on a natural language to communicate technical concepts in a multi-lingual environment, which is the rule rather than the exception where international standards are being developed.

Finally, they can aid standards development at the maintenance stage, by allowing (for example) the adequacy of a proposed change to a standard to be formally proved; the availability of tools such as theorem provers should help considerably in reducing maintenance costs both to standards developers and users.

It is, however, by no means self-evident that the use of a formal notation necessarily improves a standard. Even when features such as lack of ambiguity are demonstrable, the formal expression of a standard does not improve its quality if it is inaccessible to its users. With this problem in mind it may be difficult to argue a formal standard through to acceptance. (A standard does not, of course, have to contain formal notation in order for it to be inaccessible to a significant number of those whose expert knowledge it should ideally draw upon. There are many examples where obscure style and terminology have resulted in inaccessability outside a very small group.)

There may also be problems at earlier stages in the development process. In many application areas (such as document production) they have to be developed not only with expert knowledge of computer systems but also with experts in the field these systems address. For example, the people who have expert knowledge about document structures are those professionally engaged in producing documents—in traditional publishing, technical writing, secretarial work and legal practice—who cannot be expected to have a training in mathematics or computer science. In many standards areas there is a general lack of expertise within the National Bodies both to assess the technical merits of the formally described standards and to reach consensus on them.

Notwithstanding all these considerations, the central issue in assessing whether to use formal methods in any particular standard is **correctness**. The issue of correctness is fairly stated thus: without correctness there is no quality. Without formal methods the odds are against correctness. Incorrectness is by far the most intractable fault in standards of poor quality. In dire necessity the attainment of correctness must take priority over other issues, and this is still the single most important goal of formal methods. This argues strongly for the speedy introduction of formal methods into standards.

Considerable attention, however, has to be paid to the abilities of the developers of a standard, the suppliers of implementations, and the end-users, many of whom (in the short term at least) can not be expected to be conversant in formal notation nor necessarily be expected to become so.

These needs can be addressed in various ways. One is to accompany the formal specification with a natural language commentary. For example, formal specifications written in Z at IBM in Hursley are accompanied by extensive English, in order to help the reader not conversant with Z and thereby to assist in the validation of the formal specification. It is worth noting that this English is relatively precise, since it has been influenced by the formulation in Z. Format and style are crucially important.

A different strategy is to use a method which is readily understandable but has a formal underpinning: this underpinning does not need to be directly known to the user of the method. Some of the diagrammatic methods such as SSADM are moving towards this situation.

In our concern with the use of formal notation, we should not forget how important it is to use natural language clearly in standards. Some explanation will always be necessary, to help those unfamiliar with the notation to understand what is going on. In addition, there will always be some point at which an informal interpretation is needed, and the clear exposition of such interpretations is an essential part of a usable standard. The further we stray from everyday speech, the weaker are the semantic constraints imposed on terminology or symbols by the context in which they occur. Although formal notations are an extreme example, needing explicit interpretation of every symbol to be meaningful, the terminology and phraseology used in IT is already very susceptible to such misunderstanding, especially when further refined by a specialist 'in-group' developing a standard.

5.3 Phased Introduction of Formal Methods

While an arguable long-term solution to the communication problem is simply to educate a standard's potential users in formal methods, it may be in the short term that the only acceptable solution is one of the following:

(*A*) a formal standard with comprehensive annotation in natural language;

(*B*) a formal standard alongside one in (stylised) natural language; or

(*C*) formal annexes to a non-formal standard.

Solution *A* has the advantage that the standard is still expressed formally, although conciseness will be lost. In the case of solution *B* one must face the question of which standard takes precedence in the event of an inconsistency: the most acceptable solution seems to be that such a situation constitutes an error in the standard, but then one of the benefits of a formal approach, which is precisely to eliminate ambiguities and inconsistencies, has been compromised. Solution *C*, while preserving the non-formal version as the definitive standard, allows that formal techniques could have been used to develop part or all of it. It also allows that annexes describing non-intersecting parts of the standard might be expressed in different notations.

In the stage where a standard is in use, i.e. when implementations are developed and conformance-tested, it is clearly advantageous that the standard be expressed in a specification language, such as VDM-SL, which forms part of a development method. Indeed, if a proven implementation can be completely derived from the standard specification then the need for conformance testing should be eliminated. There is clearly a crucial need to develop tools alongside formal methods. Standards developers need the ability automatically to produce correct, production-quality specifications.

The gradual introduction of formal methods in appropriate areas can only be achieved through a programme of education. It may only be finally achieved when a generation of software engineers has been trained in these approaches. However, there are indications that considerable inroads are already being made, particularly in certain standards areas. For example, TTCN (see Section 4.5.2) is not fully formal, but is arguably one step better than English and, despite its inadequacies, is being extensively used. This suggests that any improvement in the direction of formality is generally popular, at least amongst certain sectors of the standards user community in some standards areas.

Appreciating the need for a gradual migration towards the full use of formal methods, the JTC1 report [ISO87] has recommended the following three phases for their introduction into standards. Reference to these phases is also made in Annex *F* of recently issued directives for the work of JTC1 [ISO89].

Phase 1 is characterised by the fact that widespread knowledge of FDTs, and experience in formal descriptions, are lacking; there may not be sufficient resources in the National Standards Bodies to produce or review formal descriptions. Thus the development of standards has to be based on the conventional natural language approaches, leading to standards where the natural language description is the definitive standard. SCs should, however, be encouraged to develop formal definitions of their standards, since these efforts may contribute to the quality of the standards by detecting defects, may provide additional understanding to readers, and will support the evolutionary introduction of FDTs.

In this phase a formal description produced by a SC that can be considered faithfully to represent a significant part of the standard or the complete standard should, it is suggested, be published as a **technical report** in order to preserve the work done and make this information available to National Bodies and Liaison Organisations. Meanwhile SCs should develop and provide educational material for the FDTs to support their widespread introduction in the National Bodies and Liaison Organisations.

Phase 2 is characterised by the fact that knowledge of FDTs and experience in formal descriptions is more widely available; National Bodies can provide enough resources to support the production of formal descriptions. However it cannot be assured that enough National Bodies can review formal descriptions in order to enable them to cast a ballot on a proposed formally described standard.

Here it is suggested that the development of standards should still be based on conventional natural language approaches, leading to standards where the natural language description is the definitive standard. However, these developments should be accompanied and supported by the development of a formal description of these standards with the objective of improving and supporting the structure, consistency, and correctness of the natural language description. A formal description, produced by a SC, that is considered to represent faithfully a significant part of the standard or the complete standard should be published as a **informative annex** to the standard.

Phase 3 is characterised by the fact that a widespread knowledge of FDTs may be assumed; National Bodies can provide sufficient resources both to produce and review formal descriptions, and assurance exists that the application of FDTs does not unnecessarily restrict freedom of the implementations. In this phase the suggestion is that SCs should use FDTs routinely to develop their standards, and the FDT(s) used should become part of the standard together with natural language descriptions. In cases where more than one description of a given standard or part of a standard is provided, the SC must provide an indication in the standard as to which description should be treated as the definitive version.

It is suggested that whenever a discrepancy is detected between a natural language description and a formal description, or between two formal descriptions, it should be resolved by changing or improving the natural language description or the FDTs without necessarily giving preference to one over the other(s).

Under this system of guidelines a NWI proposal would need to indicate which of the above phases of development is applicable.

The JTC1 position was arrived at after considerable debate. It is not universally accepted, and it is difficult to envisage its universal uptake in the short term. It must be borne in mind that formal methods have not yet been widely introduced and that there is a global scarcity of expertise in their use. Many practitioners will consider the JTC1 recommendations to be too strong simply through a lack of familiarity with formal methods and ignorance of their potential benefits. Others will feel that the scarcity of expertise has resource implications which make some of the recommendations unrealistic. It certainly seems that a stronger position would have been premature at present. However, it is the view of the BCS Working Group that the JTC1 recommendations represent a realistic and reasonable compromise and that they should be welcomed as a step in the right direction and implemented in practice.

5.4 Parallel and Retrospective Application of Formal Methods

Ideally, a formal development might be undertaken as an integral part of the process of developing a standard, in parallel with other activities. The retrospective application of formal methods may, however, be necessary where an existing, possibly widely used, natural-language standard requires updating and clarification.

This retrospective application of formal methods is particularly problematical. Ruggles & Yee [Rug87b], for example, have raised some general issues in respect of a possible formal update to the ISO graphics standard GKS. In attempting to specify parts of the standard formally, they uncovered many deficiencies in the original natural language standard, such as insufficient abstraction and lack of hierarchical structure in the underlying data model, ambiguities, and confusing and misleading nomenclature. They were repeatedly forced to make policy decisions in order to overcome these deficiencies and proceed with the formal definition.

Thus in order to develop retrospectively a formal definition of an existing non-formal standard, numerous policy decisions need to be made in order to overcome the deficiencies which are uncovered along the way. Such decisions will of course be of no value unless successfully argued through the standards review process. A reversal of a single decision may lead to extensive changes, so it is desirable that the formal development does not proceed too far beyond the review process. On the other hand it dare not lag too far behind, lest crucial issues fail to be identified before it is too late to consider them in the review.

The FODA development was in principle a retrospective application of an FDT to an existing standard. The ISO group working on FODA did not intend to add new ideas or concepts to the ODA standard itself; they limited their work item to the formalisation of the natural English specifications of the standard's text. However, since the work on FODA was started before the ODA standard was finished in late 1988, the group was able to make some valuable contributions during the development phase. The formalisation process revealed a number of errors, inconsistencies and ambiguities in the natural English text which could then be corrected before the publication of the ODA standard. Unfortunately, not all parts of the ODA standard had been covered by FODA by the time of their publication, and ongoing work is likely to reveal further problems with the standard's text, leading to further revisions of the standard.

Problems such as these suggest that, in most cases, it might be more sensible simply to abandon a non-formal standard and start again from scratch. This view is reinforced by the fact that exercises in retrospective formalisation tend to reveal such a lack of conceptual integrity and clarity in an existing standard that the revised standard would bear little resemblance to the original anyway.

5.5 Choice of Formal Notation

Standards expressed in formal notation have the potential to be clear, unambiguous and concise in a way that even the best use of natural language cannot attain. However, it is not necessarily the case that the use of a formal notation improves a standard. Skills in the application area are as essential as skills in the use of a formal notation. Application experts must therefore work closely with formal methods experts, and it is therefore essential that they agree on the notation to be used.

Any chosen notation must itself be formally defined. This immediately raises the problem of where and how this is done. The question here is not so much technical as organisational in that the notation must be defined in such a way that a standard making use of it will be soundly based. This requires at least the editorial quality of a standard itself. The question is then whether a notation should be defined within the standard that makes use of it or whether it should be defined as a standard in its own right.

Both approaches have been tried. Thus, on the one hand, a subset of IMCL is defined as needed within the ODA standard (ISO 8613-10). On the other hand, LOTOS and Estelle are the subject of their own standards and can therefore be used as required in any OSI standard. Similarly, VDM-SL is currently in the process of standardisation and can then be used as required in other standards, such as Modula-2. If one insists that every formal notation used in standards is itself made the subject of an independent standard, then the problem of proliferating notations is held in check. However, the notation must be of wide applicability in order to justify this approach. The approach at the opposite extreme, namely customising a notation for each particular application, may pay dividends if the application is highly specialised and the notation will lead to particular clarity and conciseness. The danger with this approach is that a standard may become inaccessible to all but those people who have acquired a working facility in both the subject area and the formal notation.

In making a choice of notation, the following points should be considered.

- **Does the application really need formal notation?** If all that is needed is to state something clearly, then a great deal may be achieved with good natural language. However, if, for example, correctness is critical then natural language will be inadequate. In some intermediate circumstances a semi-formal technique might be the most appropriate.

- **If formal notation is needed, what should be the underlying mathematical basis?** For example, a logic-based technique proved useful for FODA, but would have been less useful for OSI protocols. It may be the case that different techniques are needed in order to describe different parts of an application. Decisions in this area are technically demanding and need expertise in both the application area and the range of formal techniques available.

- **What style of presentation should be adopted?** Graphical notations can be formally defined and in some cases may be the most suitable. Otherwise, the syntax of a notation should be devised with great care. (It has been remarked that LOTOS really stands for 'lots of terribly obscure symbols' because even experts can find it difficult to read!) If the semantics is right then the syntax can be varied in order to achieve a variety of presentation styles. The aim should be simplicity rather than formal minimality: the notation should be readily sight-readable.

- **Is the formal notation explicable?** No formal notation is self-explanatory—even to bullish mathematicians. A tutorial introduction in the form of a non-binding annex to the standard is highly recommended. Natural-language notes in context also aid understanding. In many cases the best option of all is a natural language text developed in parallel with a formal specification.

The choice of formal specification technique can make passions run high. Perhaps this is because most techniques take the form of languages and, as human beings, we are capable of developing strong attachments to the ways in which we express things. This produces a kind of gut-feeling politics which can permeate standards committees, particularly at international level. Hopefully this will come to be regarded as an adolescent phase. Certainly the choice of formal method should be guided predominantly by 'hard' technical considerations rather than political ones.

5.6 Tools

For software and system houses, the appearance of a standard is the enabling event to allow production of suites of tools or the incorporation of support for the new standard into existing tools product sets. The standard sharply reduces the risk of rework and allows a market analysis to be carried out to assess demand in the areas where the standard is or may become mandatory. For industry users, the appearance of the standard allows intercept and migration strategies to be produced, where the lead-time for availability of production-quality tools can be estimated and interim use of prototype tools for training and familiarisation can be planned. Programming language standards may be regarded as specifications for software engineering tools [Mee86; Mee88].

An important strategy in software development is the use of **prototypes**, which give the user a direct experience of the intended system, which they would find difficult to obtain from reading the specification. If the requirements specification has an **executable** representation (such as Prolog in the case of FODA), this gives a prototype which mirrors the specification, and thus avoids the difficulties of some prototyping approaches which still produce a written specification which is totally inscrutable to the user.

It would be generally beneficial if standards could also be progressed through trial use of a prototyping nature, as was done by the editor of the SGML standard. If formally specified there could be some hope that they could be animated in some way to help users assess the potential usefulness of the standard.

The use of an FDT in expressing a standard should provide the potential to reduce the development time of implementations by using tools that are based on the properties of the FDT itself. It should also be possible to make the conformance testing of implementations of a standard itself a formal (and possibly an automatic) process, either through formal proof or through testing where the test cases and similar have formal relationships with the standard. The existence of suitable theorem provers is crucial to the former option.

5.7 General Conclusions

The social effects of many developments in information technology are large and will continue to grow. This places the highest demands on the professionals responsible for the developments. The consequences of poor engineering could be extensive.

Technical complexity has taken natural language specification to limits at which it breaks down. A formal notation, on the other hand, may serve several useful purposes:

- it may facilitate exact description;

- it may provide a basis for the verification of the properties of the application it describes; and

- it may provide a basis for the development of tests of conformance and even demonstrably conformant implementations.

There is, however, no single formal notation which serves all of these purposes equally well for all applications. For a given application, the choice of formal notation must take into account

- the mathematical basis of the notation;

- the availability of expertise in both the application and the proposed notation;

- the purposes that the notation is intended to serve; and

- in relevant cases, the availability or feasibility of support tools.

Formal methods hold a great deal of promise for the development and use of standards as for the development and use of software. The quality of both should be enhanced through their use. The most frequently reported benefit of formal methods in the development of standards is the early detection of errors, especially if a formal description is developed in parallel with a natural language text.

Formal methods are, however, still in their youth, and there are several continuing difficulties, both technical and circumstantial. It is not uncommon, for example, to encounter vehement opposition to their use. Perhaps part of the reason is that much has been claimed for formal methods that has yet to be achieved.

In the long term there is no alternative to the use of formal methods. In the same way as we would not nowadays build bridges without prior mathematical modelling studies, so in the next century we will not build major software systems without using formal methods at every stage.

In the foreseeable future, however, a pragmatic approach is needed to issues and trade-offs. For example, formal standards have severe problems of acceptability if the public at large is expected to use them, with the result that overall quality could be severely compromised by their use. User-friendly presentations of the notations, or the use of them in the background underpinning the standard, are essential.

During the years to come, close collaboration needs to be fostered between industry, the standards community and the research community as formal methods suitable for use in standards work continue to be developed and must themselves be standardised. Suitable tools to accompany these methods are essential.

The development of tutorial and educational materials will help to provide widespread understanding of the complexities of formal methods, although time must be permitted for their assimilation.

The use of formal methods is not the only tactic that we have to enhance the quality of standards, and the overall standards-making process should seek other methods as well. However, it rejects formal methods at its peril.

Bibliography

Bibliography of Standards

ANSI/IEEE 729
    Standard glossary of software engineering terminology, IEEE, New York, 1983. Also published in the volume: *Software engineering standards*, IEEE, Wiley-Interscience, 1987.

BS 0   *A standard for standards, Part 1: General principles of standardization*, BSI, London, 1981.

CCITT T.410 Series of Recommendations
    Office Document Architecture (ODA) and Interchange Format, CCITT, Geneva, 1988 (cf. ISO 8613).

CCITT X.409
    Information Processing Systems—Open Systems Interconnection—Specification for Abstract Syntax Notation One (ASN.1), CCITT, Geneva, 1988 (cf. ISO 8824).

CCITT Z.100-Z.104
    Specification and Description Language, CCITT, Geneva, 1988.

DIN 66253 *Programming Language PEARL—Part 2: Full Language*, DIN, Berlin, 1980.

ENV 41-204
    Information Processing Systems—Open Systems Interconnection—File transfer, access and management. Simple file transfer (unstructured), CEN/CENELEC, Brussels, 1988 (cf. ISO 8571).

ISO 1538 *Information Processing Systems—Programming Languages—Algol 60*, ISO, Geneva, 1984.

ISO 1539 *Information Processing Systems—Programming Languages—FORTRAN*, ISO, Geneva, 1980, revision under preparation.

ISO 1989 *Information Processing Systems—Programming Languages—COBOL*, ISO, Geneva, 1985.

ISO 6373 *Information Processing Systems—Programming Languages—Minimal BASIC*, ISO, Geneva, 1984.

ISO 6522 *Information Processing Systems—Programming Languages—General purpose PL/I*, ISO, Geneva, 1985.

ISO 7185 *Information Processing Systems—Programming Languages—Pascal*, ISO, Geneva, 1983 (=BS 6192).

ISO 7846 *Information Processing Systems—Programming Languages—Industrial real-time FORTRAN*, ISO, Geneva, 1985 (=BS 6831).

ISO 7942   *Information Processing Systems—Computer Graphics—Graphical Kernel System (GKS) functional description*, ISO, Geneva, 1985 (=BS 6390).

ISO 8485   *Information Processing Systems—Programming Languages—APL*, ISO, Geneva, under preparation.

ISO 8571   *Information Processing Systems—Open Systems Interconnection:—File transfer, access and management (FTAM)*, ISO, Geneva, 1988 (five parts).

ISO 8613   *Office Document Architecture (ODA) and Interchange Format*, ISO, Geneva, 1988, 1989 and under preparation (ten parts).

ISO 8632   *Information Processing Systems—Computer Graphics—Metafile for the storage and transfer of picture description information (CGM)*, ISO, Geneva, 1987 (four parts) (=BS 6945).

ISO 8651   *Information Processing Systems—Computer Graphics—Graphical Kernel System (GKS) language bindings*, ISO, Geneva, 1988 and under preparation (four parts).

ISO 8652   *Information Processing Systems—Programming Languages—Ada*, ISO, Geneva, 1987.

ISO 8805   *Information Processing Systems—Computer Graphics—Graphical Kernel System for Three Dimensions (GKS-3D) functional description*, ISO, Geneva, 1988.

ISO 8806   *Information Processing Systems—Computer Graphics—Graphical Kernel System for Three Dimensions (GKS-3D) language bindings*, ISO, Geneva, under preparation (four parts).

ISO 8807   *Information Processing Systems—Open Systems Interconnection—LOTOS, a formal description technique based on the temporal ordering of observational behaviour*, ISO, Geneva, under preparation.

ISO 8824   *Information Processing Systems—Open Systems Interconnection—Specification for Abstract Syntax Notation One (ASN.1)*, ISO, Geneva, 1988 (=BS 6962).

ISO 8825   *Information Processing Systems—Open Systems Interconnection—Specification for basic encoding rules for Abstract Syntax Notation One (ASN.1)*, ISO, Geneva, 1988 (=BS 6963).

ISO 8879   *Information Processing Systems—Text and Office Systems—Standard Generalized Markup Language (SGML)* ISO, Geneva, 1986 (=BS 6868).

ISO 9074   *Information Processing Systems—Open Systems Interconnection—Estelle, a formal description technique based on an extended state transition model*, ISO, Geneva, under preparation.

ISO 9496   *Information Processing Systems—Programming Languages—CHILL*, ISO, Geneva, under preparation.

ISO 9592   *Information Processing Systems—Computer Graphics—Programmer's Hierarchical Interactive Graphics System (PHIGS)*, ISO, Geneva, 1989 (three parts) (=BS 7217).

ISO 9593   *Information Processing Systems—Computer Graphics—Programmer's Hierarchical Interactive Graphics System (PHIGS) language bindings*, ISO, Geneva, under preparation (four parts).

ISO 9636   *Information Processing Systems—Computer Graphics—Inter-
            face techniques for dialogues with graphical devices (CGI)*, ISO,
            Geneva, under preparation (six parts).

ISO 9637   *Information Processing Systems—Computer Graphics—Inter-
            face techniques for dialogues with graphical devices (CGI) lan-
            guage bindings*, ISO, Geneva, under preparation (four parts).

ISO 9646   *Information Processing Systems—Open Systems Interconnec-
            tion—Conformance testing methodology and framework*, ISO,
            Geneva, under preparation (five parts).

ISO 9899   *Information Processing Systems—Programming Languages—C*,
            ISO, Geneva, under preparation.

ISO 10167   *Information Processing Systems—Open Systems Interconnec-
            tion—Guidelines for the application of Estelle, LOTOS and SDL*,
            ISO, Geneva, under preparation.

ISO 10279   *Information Processing Systems—Programming Languages—
            BASIC*, ISO, Geneva, under preparation.

General Bibliography

[Abr80a]   J-R. Abrial, *The specification language Z: syntax and "semantics"*,
           Software Engineering Project Paper, Programming Research
           Group, Computing Laboratory, University of Oxford, April 1980.

[Abr80b]   J-R. Abrial, S.A. Schuman & B. Meyer, 'Specification language', in
           R.H. McKeag & A.M. Macnaghten (eds.), *On the construction of
           programs*, Cambridge University Press, 1980, 343-410.

[ACA86]   Cabinet Office: Advisory Committee for Applied Research and De-
           velopment, *Software: a vital key to UK competitiveness*, HMSO
           Stationery Office, 1986.

[Alf77]   M.W. Alford, 'A requirements engineering methodology for real-
           time processing requirements', *IEEE Transactions on Software
           Engineering*, **SE-3**, 60-69, 1977.

[Alf80]   M.W. Alford, 'Software Requirements Engineering Methodology
           (SREM) at the age of four', *Proceedings of COMPSAC 80*,
           Chicago, Illinois, 1980, 866-874.

[Amb86]   A.L. Ambler, D.I. Good, J.C. Browne, W.F. Burger, R.M. Cohen,
           C.G. Hoch & R.E. Wells, 'GYPSY: a language for specification and
           implementation of verifiable programs', in [Geh86].

[And82]   D.J. Andrews & W. Henhapl, 'Pascal', in [Bjø82], 175-252.

[And88]   D.J. Andrews, 'Report from the BSI panel for the standardisation
           of VDM', in [Blo88], 74-78.

[ANS82]   ANSI X3H3 Computer Graphics Standards Committee, *American
           National Standard functional specification of the Programmer's
           Minimal Interface for Graphics*, ANSI Document X3H3/82-15rl,
           1982.

[App88a]   W. Appelt, 'FODA—the formal specification of ODA document
           structures and its use as a basis for conformance testing', *Computer
           Standards and Interfaces*, **7**, 377-385, 1988.

[App88b] W. Appelt, R. Carr & G. Richter, 'The formal specification of doc-
          ument structures of the ODA standard', in *Proceedings of the EP88
          conference*, Electronic Publishing.

[Arn87]   D.B. Arnold, D.A. Duce & G.J. Reynolds, 'An approach to the
          formal specification of configurable models of graphics systems', in
          G. Maréchal (ed.), *Proceedings of Eurographics 87*, North-Hol-
          land, 1987.

[Bac59]   J.W. Backus, 'The syntax and semantics of the proposed inter-
          national algebraic language', in *Proceedings of the international
          conference on information processing*, UNESCO, Zurich, 1959,
          125-132.

[Bac78]   J. Backus, 'Can programming be liberated from the von Neumann
          style? A functional style and its algebra of programs' (Turing
          Lecture), *Communications of the ACM*, **21**(8), 613-641, 1978.

[Bat86]   G. Bate, 'Mascot 3: an informal introductory tutorial', *Software
          Engineering Journal*, **1**(3), 95-102, 1986.

[Bek74]   H. Bekic, D. Bjørner, W. Henhapl, C.B. Jones & P. Lucas, *A
          formal definition of a PL/I subset*, Technical Report 25.139, IBM
          Laboratory, Vienna, December 1974.

[Bel77]   T.E. Bell, D.C. Bixler & M.E. Dyer, 'An extendible approach to
          computer-aided software requirements engineering', *IEEE Trans-
          actions on Software Engineering*, **SE-3**, 49-60, 1977.

[Ben80]   J. Bendl, P. Koves & P. Szeredi, 'The MProlog system', in *Pro-
          ceedings of the Logic Programming Workshop*, Debrecen, Hun-
          gary, 1980.

[Ben87]   D. Benyon & S. Skidmore, 'Towards a tool kit for the systems
          analyst', *Computer Journal*, **30**(1), 2-7, 1987.

[Ber83]   D. Bert, 'Refinements of generic specifications with algebraic
          tools,' in *Proceedings of the IFIP 9th World Computer Congress*,
          Paris, September 1983, 815-820.

[Ber86]   D. Bert & R. Echahed, 'Design and implementation of a generic,
          logic and functional programming language', in B. Robinet & R.
          Wilhelm (eds.) *ESOP 86: Proceedings of the European Symposium
          on Programming, Saarbrücken, Federal Republic of Germany,
          March 17-19, 1986* (LNCS 213), Springer-Verlag, 1986, 119-132.

[Bie79]   J. Biewald, P. Goehner, R. Lauber & H. Schelling, 'EPOS—a spec-
          ification and design technique for computer controlled real-time
          automation systems', in *Proceedings of the Fourth International
          Conference on Software Engineering*, IEEE Computer Society,
          1979, 245-250.

[Bjø80]   D. Bjørner & O.N. Oest (eds.), *Towards a formal description of
          Ada* (LNCS 98), Springer-Verlag, 1980.

[Bjø82]   D. Bjørner & C.B. Jones, *Formal specification and software devel-
          opment*, Prentice-Hall, 1982.

[Bjø84]   D. Bjørner (ed.), *Formal software development methods: combin-
          ing specification methods*, Nyborg, 1984.

[Bjø87]   D. Bjørner, C.B. Jones, M. Mac an Airchinnigh & E.J. Neuhold (eds.), *VDM '87: VDM—a formal method at work* (LNCS 252), Springer-Verlag 1987.

[Blo88]   R. Bloomfield, L.S. Marshall & R. Jones (eds.), *VDM '88: VDM—the way ahead*, Springer-Verlag (LNCS 328), 1988.

[Böh79]   B. Böhm, 'Software Engineering—as it is', in *Proceedings of the Fourth International Conference on Software Engineering*, IEEE Computer Society, 1979.

[Bol88]   T. Bolognesi & H. Brinksma, 'Introduction to the ISO specification language LOTOS', *Computer Networks and ISDN Systems*, 14(1), 25-29, 1988.

[Bor88]   A. Borzyszkowski & S. Sokolowski, 'Understanding an informal description: Office Documents Architecture, an ISO standard', in [Blo88], 48-63.

[BPI89]   British Printing Industries Federation, *Printers' Yearbook 1989/90*, London, 1989.

[Bra82]   B. Brass, F. Erhart, A. Horsch, H.O. Riethmayer & R. Steinbruggan, *CIP-S: an instrument for program transformation and rule generation*, Report I.8211, Technical University of Munich, 1982.

[Bro82]   K. W. Brodlie & G. E. Pfaff, 'Report on the EEC workshop on graphics certification', *Computer Graphics Forum*, 1(3), 88-90, 1982.

[Bro84]   M.L. Brodie, J. Mylopoulos & J.W. Schmidt (eds.), *On conceptual modelling: perspectives from artificial intelligence, databases, and programming languages*, Springer-Verlag, 1984.

[Bry88]   M. Bryan, *SGML for authors*, Addison-Wesley, 1988.

[Bud87]   S. Budkowski, 'Estelle Tutorial', in *Proceedings of the 7th International Conference on Protocol Specification, Testing and Verification*, Zurich, 1987.

[Bur77]   R.M. Burstall & J.A. Goguen, 'Putting theories together to make specifications', in *Proceedings of the fifth International Joint Conference on artificial intelligence, Cambridge, Massachusetts, United States, 22-25 August 1977* (2 volumes), Carnegie-Mellon University, Pittsburgh, 1977, 1045-1058.

[Bur80a] R.M. Burstall & J.A. Goguen, 'The semantics of CLEAR, a specification language', in D. Bjørner (ed.), *Abstract software specifications* (LNCS 86), Springer-Verlag, 1980, 292-332.

[Bur80b] R.M. Burstall, D.B. MacQueen & D.T. Sannella, 'HOPE: an experimental applicative language', in *Conference record of the 1980 LISP conference: papers presented at Stanford University, Stanford, California, August 25-27, 1980*, Palo Alto, 1980, 136-143.

[Bur81]   R.M. Burstall & J.A. Goguen, 'An informal introduction to specifications using Clear', in R.S. Boyer & J. Strother Moore (eds.), *The correctness problem in computer science*, Academic Press, 1981, 185-213.

[Bus88]   D.W. Bustard, M.T. Norris & R.A. Orr, 'A pictorial approach to the animation of process-oriented formal specifications', *Software Engineering Journal*, 3(4), 114-118, 1988.

[Cam78]   I.M. Campos & G. Estrin, 'Concurrent software design supported by SARA at the age of one', *Proceedings of the 3rd International Conference on Software Engineering*, Atlanta, Georgia, 1978, 230-242.

[Cam89]   J.R. Cameron, *JSP and JSD: the Jackson approach to software development*, IEEE Computer Society Press, 1989 (second edition).

[Car83a] G. S. Carson & E. Post, *The formal specification of a computer graphics system*, Technical Report 83-6, GSC Associates, 1983.

[Car83b] G. S. Carson, The specification of computer graphics systems, *IEEE Computer Graphics and Applications*, **3**(6), 27-41, 1983.

[Cha84]   F.B. Chambers, D.A. Duce & G.P. Jones (eds.), *Distributed computing*, Academic Press, 1984.

[Che81]   M.H. Cheheyl, M. Gasser, G.A. Huff & J.K. Miller, 'Verifying security', *ACM Computing Surveys*, **13**(3), 279-339, 1981.

[Chu36]   A. Church, 'An unsolvable problem in elementary number theory', *American Journal of Mathematics*, **58**, 345-363, 1936.

[Cla83]   K.L. Clark & S. Gregory, *PARLOG: A parallel logic programming language*, Research Report DOC 83/5, Department of Computing, Imperial College, University of London, 1983.

[Cle77]   J. Cleaveland & R.C. Uzgalis, *Grammars for programming languages*, Elsevier, New York, 1977.

[Clo81]   W.F. Clocksin & C.S. Mellish, *Programming in Prolog*, Springer-Verlag, 1981.

[Clo84]   W.F. Clocksin, 'Logic programming and Prolog', in [Cha84], 79-109.

[Coh86]   B. Cohen, W. Harwood & M. Jackson, *The specification of complex systems*, Addison-Wesley, 1986.

[Col84]   D. Coleman & R. M. Gallimore, *Software engineering using executable specification*, Department of Computation, UMIST, 1984.

[Col87]   D. Coleman, R.M. Gallimore & V. Stavridou, 'The design of a rewrite rule interpreter from algebraic specifications', *Software Engineering Journal*, **2**(4), 95-104, 1987.

[Cot85]   I.D. Cottam, C.B. Jones, T. Nipkow, A.C. Wills, M.I. Wolczko & A. Yaghi, 'Project support environments for formal methods', in J.A. McDermid (ed.), *Integrated project support environments*, Peter Peregrinus, 1985, 32-53.

[Dar82]   J. Darlington, P. Henderson & D.A. Turner (eds.), *Functional programming and its applications*, Cambridge University Press, 1982.

[Dar84]   J. Darlington, 'Functional programming', in [Cha84], 57-77.

[Das85]   B. Dasarathy, 'Timing constraints of real-time systems: constructs for expressing them, methods of validating them', *IEEE Transactions on Software Engineering*, **SE-11**, 80-86, 1985.

[Dec88]   O. Declerfayt, B. Demeuse, F. Wautier, P-Y. Schobbens & E. Milgrom, 'Precise standards through formal specifications: a case study: the UNIX file system', *Proceedings of the EUUG Autumn 1988 Conference*, Cascais, Portugal, 1988.

[DeM78]   T. De Marco, *Structured analysis and system specification*, Yourdon Press, 1978.

[Dow88]   E. Downs, P. Clare & I. Coe, *Structured systems analysis and design method application and context*, Prentice-Hall, 1988.

[Duc82]   D. A. Duce, 'The EEC workshop on formal specification of graphics software standards', *Computer Graphics Forum*, **1**(3) 92-95, 1982.

[Duc84]   D.A. Duce, E.V.C. Fielding & L.S. Marshall, *Formal specification and graphics software*, Technical Report RAL-84-068, Rutherford Appleton Laboratories, Chilton, Didcot, Oxon., 1984.

[Duc85]   D.A. Duce & E.V.C. Fielding, 'Better understanding through formal specification', *Computer Graphics Forum*, **4**(4), 333-348, 1985.

[Duc86a] D.A. Duce & E.V.C. Fielding, 'Formal specification—a simple example', *ICL Technical Journal*, **5**(1), 96-111, 1986.

[Duc86b] D. A. Duce & E. V. C. Fielding, 'Towards a formal specification of the GKS output primitives', in [Req86].

[Duc86c] D. A. Duce & F. R. A. Hopgood, *Compatibility between GKS-3D and PHIGS*, Document IST/21/2/3: 15, BSI, London, 1986.

[Duc87a] D. A. Duce & E. V. C. Fielding, 'Formal specification—a comparison of two techniques', *Computer Journal*, **30**(4), 316-327, 1987.

[Duc87b] D. A. Duce, F. R. A. Hopgood, C. L. N. Ruggles & S. T. Yee, *Input in GKS—a discussion paper*, Technical Report RAL-87-057, Rutherford Appleton Laboratory, Chilton, Didcot, Oxon., 1987.

[Duc87c] D. A. Duce & M. S. Parsons, 'GKS—Some lessons learnt from formal specification', in W.T. Hewitt (ed.), *Proceedings of the GKS review workshop*, Eurographics Association, 1987.

[Duc88]   D. A. Duce, E. V. C. Fielding & L. S. Marshall, 'Formal specification of a small example based on GKS', *Transactions on Graphics* **7**(3), 180-197, 1988.

[Duc89a] D. A. Duce, 'GKS, structures and formal specification', in [Han89].

[Duc89b] D. A. Duce, P. J. W. ten Hagen & R. van Liese, 'Components, frameworks and GKS input', in [Han89].

[Eck80]   R. Eckert, 'Specification of graphics systems', in R. A. Guedj, P. J. W. ten Hagen, F. R. A. Hopgood, H. Tucker & D. A. Duce (eds.), *Proceedings of the IFIP workshop on methodology of interaction*, North-Holland, 1980, 195-209.

[Ehr82]   H. Ehrig, H.J. Kreowski, B. Mahr & P. Padawitz, 'Algebraic implementation of abstract data types', *Theoretical Computer Science*, **20**(3), 209-263, 1982.

[Ehr83]   H. Ehrig, W. Fey & H. Hansen, *ACT ONE—an algebraic specification language with two levels of semantics*, Technical Report 83-03, Technical University of Berlin, 1983.

[Ehr85]   H. Ehrig & B. Mahr, *Fundamentals of algebraic specification, 1: Equations and initial semantics* (EATCS Monographs on Theoretical Computer Science, 6), Springer-Verlag, 1985.

[Ehr86]   H. Ehrig & H. Weber, 'Programming in the large with algebraic module specification', in [Kug86].

[Ehr88]   H. Ehrig & P. Pepper, 'On the potential role of algebraic specifi-
          cation within computer science', *Bulletin of the EATCS*, **35**, 69-
          71, 1988.

[Eis87]   S. Eisenbach (ed.), *Functional programming: languages, tools and
          architectures,* Ellis Horwood Press, 1987.

[Fid86]   M. Fidelak, 'Petri Nets: a formal language for knowledge rep-
          resentation', in *Proceedings of the 7th European Conference on
          Artificial Intelligence*, Brighton (UK), Volume 2, 1986, 164-168.

[Fut85]   K. Futatsugi, J.A. Goguen, J.P. Jouannaud & J. Meseguer, 'Prin-
          ciples of OBJ2', *Proceedings of the 1985 Symposium on Principles
          of Programming Languages*, 1985.

[Gan79]   C. Gane & T. Sarson, *Structured systems analysis, tools and tech-
          niques*, Prentice-Hall, 1979.

[Geh86]   N. Gehani & A.D. McGettrick (eds.), *Software specification tech-
          niques*, Addison-Wesley, 1986.

[Gen88]   Generics Software Ltd., *GenASSIST*, Product Literature, Dublin,
          Ireland, 1988.

[Ger87]   Gerrard Software Ltd., *ObjEx: An Introduction*, Product Liter-
          ature, Macclesfield, Cheshire, England, 1987.

[Gna83]   R. Gnatz, 'An algebraic approach to the standardisation and the
          certification of graphics software', *Computer Graphics Forum*,
          2(2/3), 153-166, 1983.

[Gog79]   J.A. Goguen & J.J. Tardo, 'An introduction to OBJ: a language for
          writing and testing formal algebraic program specifications', in
          Proceedings of the conference on specification of reliable software,
          IEEE Computer Society, 1979, 170-189.

[Gog82]   J.A. Goguen & J. Meseguer, 'Rapid prototyping in the OBJ exe-
          cutable specification language', *ACM Sigsoft Software Engineering
          Notes* **7**(5), 75-84, 1982.

[Gol80]   N. Goldman & D. Wile, 'A relational database foundation for pro-
          cess specification', in *Entity-relationship approach to systems
          analysis and design*, North-Holland, 1980, 413-432.

[Gom84]   H. Gomaa, 'A software design method for real-time systems', *Com-
          munications of the ACM*, **27**(9), 938-949, 1984.

[Gom86]   H. Gomaa, 'Software development of real-time systems', *Com-
          munications of the ACM*, **29**(7), 657-668, 1986.

[Goo79]   D.I. Good, R.M. Cohen & J. Keeton-Williams, 'Principles of
          proving concurrent programs in Gypsy', in *Proceedings of the 6th
          ACM POPL Symposium*, San Antonio, Texas, 1979.

[Gor79a] M.J. Gordon, A.J.R.G. Milner & C.P. Wadsworth, *Edinburgh
          LCF: a mechanised logic of computation* (LNCS 78), Springer-
          Verlag, 1979.

[Gor79b] M.J.C. Gordon, *The denotational description of programming
          languages, an introduction*, Springer-Verlag, 1979.

[GSP79]   GSPC, 'Status report on the graphic standards planning committee',
          Computer Graphics **13**(3), 1– V-10 (entire volume), 1979.

[Gut80]   J. Guttag & J.J. Horning, 'Formal specification as a design tool', in *Proceedings of the Seventh Annual ACM Symposium on Principles of Programming Languages*, 1980, 251-261.

[Gut85a] J.V. Guttag, J.J. Horning & J.M. Wing, *Larch in five easy lessons*, Technical report 5, Digital Equipment Corporation Systems Research Center, 1985.

[Gut85b] J.V. Guttag, J.J. Horning & J.M. Wing, 'The Larch family of specification languages', *IEEE Software*, **2**(5), 24-36, 1985.

[Hac79]   W.R. Hackler & A. Samarov, *An AXES specification of a radar scheduler*, Technical Report 23, Higher Order Software, Inc., Cambridge, Mass., USA, November 1979.

[Ham76a] M. Hamilton & S. Zeldin, *Integrated software development system—Higher Order Software conceptual description*, Technical Report 3, Higher Order Software, Inc., Cambridge, Mass., USA, November 1976.

[Ham76b] M. Hamilton & S. Zeldin, 'Higher Order Software—A methodology for defining software', *IEEE Transactions on Software Engineering*, **SE-2**, 9-32, 1976.

[Han89]   W. Hansmann, F. R. A. Hopgood & W. Strasser (eds.), *Proceedings of the Eurographics '89 conference*, North-Holland, 1989.

[Har87]   D. Harel, 'State Charts: A visual formalism for complex systems', *Science of Computer Programming*, **8**, 231-274, 1987.

[Har88]   D. Harel, 'On visual formalisms', *Communications of the ACM*, **31**(5), 514-530, 1988.

[Hat87]   D.J. Hatley & I.A. Pirbhai, *Strategies for real-time system specification*, Dorset House Publishing, New York, 1987.

[Hay87]   I. Hayes (ed.), *Specification case studies*, Prentice-Hall, 1987.

[Hen84]   P. Henderson, *Me too—a language for software specification and model building—Preliminary report*, Technical Report FPN-9, Department of Computing Science, University of Stirling, 1984.

[Hoa69]   C.A.R. Hoare, 'An axiomatic basis for computer programming', *Communications of the ACM*, **12**, 576-580, 1969.

[Hoa73]   C.A.R. Hoare & N. Wirth, 'An axiomatic definition of the programming language Pascal', *Acta Informatica*, **2**, 335-355, 1973.

[Hoa85a] C.A.R. Hoare, *Communicating sequential processes*, Prentice-Hall, 1985.

[Hoa85b] C.A.R. Hoare & J.C. Shepherdson (eds.), *Mathematical logic and programming languages*, Prentice-Hall, 1985.

[Hoa87]   C.A.R. Hoare, 'An overview of some formal methods for program design', *IEEE Computer*, **20**(9), 85-91, 1987.

[Hop86a] F. R. A. Hopgood, D. A. Duce, E. V. C. Fielding, K. Robinson & A. S. Williams, *Methodology of window management*, Springer-Verlag, 1986.

[Hop86b] F. R. A. Hopgood, D. A. Duce, J. R. Gallop & D. C. Sutcliffe, *Introduction to the Graphical Kernel System (GKS)*, Academic Press, 1986 (second edition).

[ILo87]   *The languages of STATEMATE*, Technical Report, i-Logix, Bur-
          lington, Mass., USA, 1987.

[Ing79]   L. Ingevaldsson, *JSP: A practical method of program design*,
          Chartwell Bratt, 1979.

[ISO]   ISO references other than those below refer to Standards and are
          listed separately in the *Bibliography of Standards* which precedes
          this *General Bibliography*.

[ISO80]   *General terms and their definitions concerning standardization and
          certification.* ISO Guide 2, Geneva, 1980.

[ISO87]   *JTC1 statement of policy on formal description techniques*,
          ISO/IEC JTC1 N145 & ISO/IEC JTC1/SC18 N1333, Geneva, 1987.

[ISO88a] *Informal guide for ISO/IEC JTC1 and CCITT cooperation*, ISO/
          IEC/JTC1 N303, Geneva, 1988.

[ISO88b] *Information processing: Text and Office Systems: strategy for stan-
          dards development*, ISO/IEC JTC1/SC 18/WG3 N1086, Geneva,
          1988.

[ISO89]   *Directives for the work of ISO/IEC Joint Technical Committee 1
          (JTC1) on Information Technology*, ISO/ IEC JTC1 N535, Geneva,
          1989.

[Jac75]   M.A. Jackson, *Principles of program design*, Academic Press,
          1975.

[Jac83]   M.A. Jackson, *System development*, Prentice-Hall, 1983.

[Jon80]   C.B. Jones, *Software development: a rigorous approach*, Prentice-
          Hall, 1980.

[Jon83]   C.B. Jones, 'Specification and design of (parallel) programs', in
          [Mas83], 321-332.

[Jon86]   C.B. Jones, *Systematic software development using VDM*, Pren-
          tice-Hall, 1986.

[Jon88]   C.B. Jones & P.A. Lindsay, 'A support system for formal reason-
          ing: requirements and status', in [Blo88], 139-152.

[Kar88]   G. Karam, *The FODA conformance analyzer: prototyping with
          Prolog*, Technical Report, Department of Computing and System
          Engineering, Carleton University, 1988.

[Kin86]   S. King, I.H. Sorensen & J. Woodcock, *A syntax for the Z notation,
          Draft 2.3*, Programming Research Group, Computing Laboratory,
          University of Oxford, November 1986.

[Kle36]   S.C. Kleene, 'General recursive functions of natural numbers',
          Mathematische Annalen, **112**, 727-742, 1936.

[Kow85]   R. Kowalski, 'The relation between logic programming and logic
          specification', in [Hoa85b], 11-27.

[Kug86]   H.-J. Kugler (ed.), *Information processing '86—Proceedings of the
          tenth IFIP World Congress, Dublin, 1986*, North-Holland, 1986.

[Les84]   P. Lescanne, 'REVE: A rewrite rule laboratory', in [Bjø84].

[Lev79]   K. Levitt, L. Robinson & B. Silverberg, *The HDM handbook, Vols.
          I, II and III*, Technical Report, Computer Science Laboratory, SRI
          International, 1979.

[Lev86]   N.G. Leveson, 'Software safety: why, what and how', *Computing Surveys*, **18**, 125-163, 1986.

[Lis86]   B. Liskov & J. Guttag, *Abstraction and specification in program development*, MIT Press, Cambridge, Mass., USA, 1986.

[McC60]   J. McCarthy, 'Recursive functions of symbolic expressions and their computation by machine', *Communications of the ACM*, **3**(4), 184-195, 1960.

[McC85]   T.J. McCabe *et al.*, 'Structured Real-Time Analysis and design', in *Proceedings of COMPSAC-85*, IEEE, 1985, 40-52.

[McG78]   A.D. McGettrick, 'An introduction to the formal definition of Algol 68', *Annual Review in Automated Programming*, **9**, 1-84, 1978.

[Mal82]   W. R. Mallgren, 'Formal specification of graphic data types', *ACM Transactions on Programming Languages and Systems*, **4**(4), 687-710, 1982.

[Mal83]   W. R. Mallgren, *Formal specification of interactive graphics programming languages* (ACM distinguished dissertation 1982), MIT press, 1983.

[Mar76]   M. Marcotty, H.F. Ledgard & G.V. Bochmann, 'A sampler of formal definitions', *ACM Computing Surveys*, **8**(2), 191-276, 1976.

[Mar84]   L.S. Marshall, *GKS output workstations: formal specification and proofs of correctness for specific devices*, Transfer report, University of Manchester, 1984.

[Mar85a] J. Martin, *System design from provably correct constructs*, Prentice-Hall, 1985.

[Mar85b] L. S. Marshall, 'A formal specification of line representation on graphics devices', in H. Ehrig, C. Floyd, M. Nivat & J.W. Thatcher (eds.), *Formal methods of software development, Volume 2: Colloquium on software engineering* (LNCS 186), Springer-Verlag, 1985, 129-147.

[Mas83]   R.E.A. Mason (ed.), *Information processing '83*, Elsevier Science Publishers B.V., North-Holland, 1983.

[May81]   B.H. Mayoh, 'Attribute grammars and mathematical semantics', *SIAM Journal of Computing*, **10**, 503-518, 1981.

[Mee86]   B. Meek, 'Programming language standards: not language definitions, but specifications of software engineering tools', in [Kug86], 301-306.

[Mee88]   B. Meek, 'Language standards committees and revisions', *ACM Sigplan Notices*, **23**(12), 134-142, 1988.

[Mid88]   C.A. Middleburg, 'The VIP VDM specification language', in [Blo88], 187-201.

[Mid89]   C.A. Middleburg, 'VVSL: a language for structured VDM specifications', *Formal Aspects of Computing*, **1**, 115-135.

[Mil76]   R. Milne & C. Strachey, *A theory of programming language semantics*, Chapman and Hall, 1976.

[Mil80]   A.J.R.G. Milner, *A calculus of communicating systems* (LNCS 92), Springer-Verlag, 1980.

[Mil86]   A.J.R.G. Milner, *Is computing an experimental science?*, Inaugural Lecture, Laboratory for the Foundations of Theoretical Computer Science, Department of Computer Science, University of Edinburgh, 1986.

[Min67]   M.L. Minsky, *Computation: finite and infinite machines*, Prentice-Hall, 1967.

[Mof88]   D.S. Moffat & P.M.D. Gray, 'Perlog: a Prolog with persistence and modules', *Computer Journal*, 31(2), 110-115, 1988.

[MSA80]   *The official handbook of MASCOT*, Mascot Suppliers Association, Malvern, UK, 1980.

[Mye78]   G.J. Myers, *Composite/Structured Design*, Van Nostrand Reinhold, 1978.

[NCC77]   *Report on standards in computing: a consultative document produced by the NCC Ltd. for the DTI*, NCC, Manchester, UK, 1977.

[NCC86]   *SSADM manual*, NCC, Manchester, UK, 1986.

[NCC87]   *The STARTS guide*, NCC, Manchester, UK, 1987 (second edition).

[New88]   J. Newport, 'Designing for method, not madness', *Parallelogram*, 3, 10-12, 1988.

[Nie89]   M. Nielsen, K. Havelund, K.R. Wagner & C. George, 'The RAISE language, method and tools', *Formal Aspects of Computing*, 1, 85-114, 1989.

[Oll74]   A. Ollengren, *Definition of programming languages by interpreting automata*, Academic Press, 1974.

[Ond87]   T. Onodera & S. Kawai, *The visualizing problem: a formalized model of visualization of graphical primitives*, Technical Report 87-22, Department of Information Science, Faculty of Science, University of Tokyo, Japan, July 1987.

[Pag80]   M. Page-Jones, *The practical guide to structured systems design*, Yourdon Press, 1980.

[Pag81]   F.G. Pagan, *Semantics of programming languages: a panoramic primer*, Prentice-Hall, 1981.

[Pet62]   C.A. Petri, *Kommunikation mit Automaten*, (Communication with Automata), PhD dissertation, University of Bonn, 1962.

[Pet81]   J.L. Peterson, *Petri net theory and the modelling of systems*, Prentice-Hall, 1981.

[Ran86]   B. Randell, 'System design and structuring', *Computer Journal*, 29(4), 300-306, 1986.

[Rea88]   C.M.P. Reade & P. Froome, 'Formal methods for reliability', Chapter 3 in *Software reliability handbook*, Addison-Wesley, 1988.

[Rei85]   W. Reisig, *Petri nets—an introduction*, Springer-Verlag, 1985.

[Req86]   A.A.G. Requicha (ed.), *Proceedings of the Eurographics '86 conference*, North-Holland, 1986.

[Rey86]   G.J. Reynolds, 'A token based graphics system', *Computer Graphics Forum* 5(2),139-146, 1986.

[Ric86]   D. Richter, 'Mappings between product data definitions', in [Req86].

[Ric88]   G. Richter & R. Durchholz, *Information modelling by compos-
           ition—the IMC/IMCL reference manual*, Technical report, GMD,
           Sankt Augustin.

[Rob77]   L. Robinson & O. Roubine, *SPECIAL, a specification and assertion
           language*, Report CSL-46, SRI International, California, USA,
           1977.

[Ros77]   D.T. Ross, 'Structured Analysis (SA): a language for commun-
           icating ideas', *IEEE Transactions on Software Engineering*, **SE-3**,
           16-34, 1977.

[Ros80]   D. S. H. Rosenthal, *A framework for specifying GKS*, ANSI Doc-
           ument X3H3/80-63, ANSI, 1980.

[Rug87a]   C.L.N. Ruggles & S.T. Yee, 'Clarification through formal specifi-
           cation: some notes on attempting a top-down formal specification of
           GKS in Meta-IV', in W.T. Hewitt (ed.), *Proceedings of the GKS
           review workshop*, Eurographics Association, 1987.

[Rug87b]   C.L.N. Ruggles & S.T. Yee, 'Notes on attempting a top-down for-
           mal specification of GKS in META-IV', Technical Report 3,
           Computing Studies Department, University of Leicester, 1987.

[Rug88]   C.L.N. Ruggles, 'Towards a formal definition of GKS and other
           graphics standards', in [Blo88], pp. 64-73.

[San82]   E. Santane-Toth & P. Szeredi, 'Prolog applications in Hungary', in
           K.L. Clark and S.-A. Tärnlund (eds.), *Logic programming*, Aca-
           demic Press, 1982, 13-31.

[Sar87]   R. Saracco & P.A.J. Tilanus, 'CCITT SDL: Overview of the lan-
           guage and its applications', *Computer Networks and ISDN Systems*,
           13(2), 65-74, 1987.

[Sch86]   S.A. Schuman & D.H. Pitt, *Object-oriented subsystem specification*,
           in L. Meertens (ed.), *Proceedings of the IFIP Working Conference
           on Program Specification and Transformation*, North-Holland,
           1986.

[Sch88]   D.A Schmidt, *Denotational semantics: a methodology for language
           development*, Wm. C. Brown Publishers, Dubuque, Iowa, USA,
           1988.

[Sim86]   H. Simpson, 'The Mascot method', *Software Engineering Journal*,
           1(3), 103-120, 1986.

[Smi88]   J.M. Smith & R. Stuteley, *SGML*, Ellis-Horwood, 1988.

[Sor81]   I. H. Sorensen, *A design of a display interface*, Programming
           Research Group, Computing Laboratory, University of Oxford,
           1981.

[SPE86]   SPECS, *Deliverable D4 Part II—IBC view of existing specification
           methods and tools—critical evaluation*, RACE Project 2039, CEC,
           Brussels, 1986.

[Spi88a]   J.M. Spivey, *Understanding Z—a specification language and its
           formal semantics*, Cambridge University Press, 1988.

[Spi88b]   J.M. Spivey, *The Z Notation—a reference manual*, Prentice-Hall,
           1988.

[Sto77]   J.E. Stoy, *Denotational semantics: the Scott-Strachey approach to programming language theory*, MIT Press, Cambridge, Mass., USA, 1977.

[Suf86]   B. Sufrin (ed.), *Z handbook, draft 1.1*, Programming Research Group, Computing Laboratory, University of Oxford, March 1986.

[Tay80]   B. Taylor, 'A method for expressing the functional requirements of real-time systems', in *Proceedings of the 9th IFAC/IFIP conference on real-time programming*, Pergamon, 1980, 111-120.

[Tur85]   D.A. Turner, 'Functional programs as executable specifications', in [Hoa85b].

[Tur87]   K.J. Turner, 'LOTOS—a practical formal description technique for OSI', in *Proceedings of the international conference on open systems*, London, 1987, 265-280.

[Var87]   V. Varadharajan & K.D. Baker, 'Directed graph based representation for software system design', *Software Engineering Journal*, 2(1), 21-28, 1987.

[War85]   P.T. Ward & S.J. Mellor, *Structured development for real time systems* (three volumes), Yourdon Press, 1985.

[Weg72a]   P. Wegner, The Vienna Definition Language, *ACM Computing Surveys*, 4, 5-63, 1972.

[Weg72b]   P. Wegner, 'Programming language semantics', in R. Rustin (ed.), *Formal semantics of programming languages*, Prentice-Hall, 1972, 149-248.

[Wij75]   A. van Wijngaarden, *Revised report on the algorithmic language Algol 68*, Springer-Verlag, 1975.

[Wik87]   A. Wikstrom, *Functional programming using ML*, Prentice-Hall, 1987.

[Wil82]   D.S. Wile, *Program developments: formal explanations of implementations*, Report RR-82-99, Information Sciences Institute, University of Southern California, 1982.

[You78]   E. Yourdon & L. Constantine, *Structured design*, Yourdon Press, 1978.

[Zil82]   S.N. Zilles, P. Lucas & J.W. Thatcher, *A look at algebraic specifications*, IBM Research Report RJ 3568, 1982.

APPENDIX A
List of Acronyms

This list of acronyms is organised alphabetically. Italicised acronyms within definitions indicate a cross-reference to an acronym defined elsewhere in the list. Italicised definitions indicate that the term concerned is defined in the accompanying glossary (Appendix *B*).

ACARD	Advisory Committee for Applied Research and Development
ACM	Association for Computing Machinery
ACP	Activity Channel Pool (in *MASCOT*)
ACSE	Association Control Service Element
AFNOR	French Association for Normalization
ANSA	Advanced Networked Systems Architecture
ANSI	American National Standards Institute
APG	*Application Program Generator*
APSE	Ada Programming Support Environment
ASN	Abstract Syntax Notation
ASPIC	Author's Standard Pre-press Interface Code
BCS	British Computer Society
BNF	*Backus-Naur Form*
BPIF	British Printing Industries Federation
BSI	British Standards Institution
CCF	*Conjunctive Canonical Form*
CCITT	International Consultative Committee for Telephony and Telegraphy
CCS	*Calculus of Communicating Systems*
CEC	Commission of the European Communities
CEN	European Committee for Standardisation
CENELEC	European Committee for Electro-Technical Standardisation

CEPT	European Conference of Postal and Telecommunications Administration
CGM	Computer Graphics Metafile
CGI	Computer Graphics Interface
CITI	Cranfield Information Technology Institute
CNF	*Conjunctive Normal Form*
COBOL	Common Business-Oriented Language
CORE	Controlled Requirements Expression
CSA	Canadian Standards Association
CSM	*Complete Sequential Machine*
CSP	*Communicating Sequential Processes*
CTS-WAN	Conformance Testing Services over Wide Area Networks
DAD	Draft Addendum
DARTS	Design Approach for Real-Time Systems
DC	Device Co-ordinate(s)
DCF	*Disjunctive Canonical Form*
DIN	Deutsches Institut für Normung
DIS	Draft International Standard
DML	Data Manipulation Language
DNF	*Disjunctive Normal Form*
DOAM	Distributed Office Application Model
DP	Draft Proposal
DSSSL	Document Style, Semantics and Specification Language
DTD	Document Type Definition
DTI	Department of Trade and Industry
EATCS	European Association for Theoretical Computer Science
EBNF	Extended *BNF*
ECMA	European Computer Manufacturers' Association
EDM	Evolutionary Design Methodology
EPOS	Entwurfsunterstutzendes PEARL-Orientirtes Spezifikationssystem
ESPRIT	European Strategic Programme for Research in Information Technology

Estelle	Extended *Finite State Machine Language*
EWOS	European Workshop on Open Systems
FDM	*Formal Development Method*
FDT	*Formal Description Technique*
FM	*Formal Method*
FODA	Formal Specification of *ODA*
FORSITE	Formal Specification of Sequential and Concurrent Systems
FSL	*Formal Specification Language*
FSM	*Finite State Machine*
FTAM	File Transfer, Access and Management
GDP	Generalised Drawing Primitive
GKS	Graphical Kernel System
GKS-3D	Graphical Kernel System for three dimensions
GMD	Gesellschaft für Mathematik und Datenverarbeitung
GSM	*Generalised Sequential Machine*
GSPC	Graphic Standards Planning Committee
HDM	Hierarchical Development Method
HIPO	Hierarchical Input-Process-Output
HOS	Higher Order Software
IBM	International Business Machines
ICI	Imperial Chemical Industries
ICL	International Computers Ltd.
IEC	International Electro-Technical Commission
IEEE	Institute of Electrical and Electronic Engineers
IFAC	International Federation of Automatic Control
IFIP	International Federation for Information Processing
IMC	Information Modelling by Composition
IMCL	Information Modelling by Composition Language
IPSE	Integrated Project Support Environment
IS	International Standard
ISAC	Information Systems work and Analysis of Changes
ISDN	Integrated Services Digital Network

ISF	Information Systems Factory
ISO	International Organisation for Standardisation
ISP	International Standard Profile
IST	Information Systems and Technology (BSI Technical Committee designation)
IT	Information Technology
JISC	Japanese Industrial Standards Committee
JSD	*Jackson System Development*
JSP	*Jackson Structured Programming*
JTC	Joint Technical Committee
LBA	*Linear Bounded Automaton*
LISP	List Processing
LNCS	Lecture Notes in Computer Science
LOTOS	*Language of Temporal Ordering Specification*
LPG	Language for Generic Programming
LUB	*Least Upper Bound*
MASCOT	Modular Approach to Software Construction, Operation and Testing
MIT	Massachusetts Institute of Technology
ML	Meta-Language
MOTIS	Message-Oriented Text Interchange System
NCC	National Computing Centre
NDC	Normalised Device Co-ordinate(s)
NHS	National Health Service
NPL	National Physical Laboratory
NWI	New Work Item
ODA	Office Document Architecture
ODIF	Office Document Interchange Format
ODP	Open Distributed Processing
OSI	Open Systems Interconnection
PAL	Presentation and Application Layers
PCCF	*Prenex Conjunctive Canonical Form*
PCF	*Prenex Canonical Form*

PCNF	*Prenex Conjunctive Normal Form*
PCO	Point of Control and Observation
PCTE	Portable Common Tool Environment
PDA	*Pushdown Automaton*
PDAD	Proposed Draft Addendum
PDCF	*Prenex Disjunctive Canonical Form*
PDNF	*Prenex Disjunctive Normal Form*
PDU	Protocol Data Unit
PEEP	Pictorial Exposition of Executing Programs
PHIGS	Programmer's Hierarchical Interactive Graphics System
PL/1	Programming Language 1
PNF	*Prenex Normal Form*
PSL/PSA	Problem Statement Language/Problem Statement Analyser
RACE	Research in Advanced Computer Electronics
RAISE	Rigorous Approach to Industrial Software Engineering
REVS	Requirements Engineering and Validation System
RSL	Requirements Statement Language
RTRL	Real-Time Requirements Language
SADT	Structured Analysis and Design Technique
SA-SD	Structured Analysis and Structured Design
SARA	System Architect's Apprentice
SC	Subcommittee
SCCS	Synchronous *CCS*
SD	System Developer
SDIF	*SGML* Document Interchange Format
SDL	System Definition Language
SDL	Specification and Description Language (of the *CCITT*)
SDM	System Development Methodology
SDS/RSRE	Software Development System
SGML	Standard Generalised Markup Language
SI	Système Internationale
SIAM	Society for Industrial and Applied Mathematics

SML   Standard *ML*

SPDL   Standard Page Description Language

SREM   Software Requirements Engineering Methodology

SRI   Stanford Research Institute

SSADM   *Structured Systems Analysis and Design Methodology*

STARTS   Software Tools for Application to Real-Time Systems

STC   Standard Telephones and Cables

STRADIS   Structured Analysis, Design and Implementation of Information Systems

SWG   Special Working Group

TC   Technical Committee

TODAC   Testing *ODA* Conformance

TOS   Text and Office Systems

TTCN   Tree and Tabular Combined Notation

UMIST   University of Manchester Institute of Science and Technology

VDL   *Vienna Definition Language*

VDM   *Vienna Development Method*

VDM-SL   *VDM* Specification Language

VIP   *VDM* for Interfaces of the *PCTE*

WC   World Co-ordinate(s)

WFF   *Well-Formed Formula*

WG   Working Group

APPENDIX B
Glossary of Formal Methods Terminology

The glossary is organised alphabetically. Entries comprise a term listed in bold followed by a definition of its principal meanings in the context of Formal Methods. The part of speech of a term is specified if it is not obvious from its everyday usage. The subject area of a definition is indicated in square brackets. Italicised words within a definition indicate cross-references to acronyms defined in the accompanying list of acronyms (Appendix A) or terms defined elsewhere in the glossary. Abbreviations used to indicate parts of speech and subject areas are listed below.

The following abbreviations are used for parts of speech:

adj	adjective
n	noun
v.i.	verb, intransitive
v.t.	verb, transitive

The following abbreviations are used for subject areas:

Alg	Algebra
Aut	Automata Theory
Com	Computation Theory
Gen	General
GNT	Graph & Net Theory
Lan	Formal Language Theory
Log	Logic
PPr	Programming Practice
PTh	Programming Theory
STh	Set Theory
SwT	Software Tools
Top	Topology

A

Abelian (adj) [Alg]: *commutative*, especially of a *group*.

Abelian Group [Alg]: a *group* with a *commutative operation*.

Abort (n) [Gen]: unsuccessful termination of a part of a program or *process*; [PTh]: a command in a *guarded command language* for which the *post-condition* is always false regardless of the *pre-condition*.

Absorption, Property of [Alg]: a property of a *Boolean algebra* such that, for all *a* and *b*, $(a + a \cdot b) = a$.

Abstract (adj) [Gen]: generalised from consideration of particular instances. Cf. *concrete*.

Abstract Data Type [Alg]: a *set* ϑ of *sets* together with *operations* on ϑ; [PTh]: a *data type* whose *operations* permit information hiding, i.e. such that all *elements* of the *sort* may be generated without any need to know how the data will be represented or how the *operations* will be implemented.

Abstract Syntax [PTh]: a form of *syntax* often used in connection with *denotational semantics* which refers to a linguistic construct in terms of the elements of which it is composed, but without regard to the *sentential forms* occurring in its *derivation* according to a *grammar*.

Abstraction: the process or result of abstracting, e.g. definition by abstraction.

Action Entry [SwT]: part of a *decision table* specifying which actions in the *action stub* are carried out for given entries in the *condition entry*.

Action Stub [SwT]: part of a *decision table* listing actions which may be carried out.

Acyclic [GNT]: a *graph* is said to be acyclic if and only if there is no *vertex v* such that there exists a *path* from *v* to itself.

Agent [PTh]: in *CCS*, the abstraction of a process or other communicating entity.

Alexandroff Topology [Top]: the *topology* on a *complete partial order* consisting of all *subsets U* which satisfy the property that, if *x* is in *U* and $x \le y$, then *y* is in *U*. Cf. *Scott topology*.

Algebra [Alg]: the branch of mathematics dealing with systems of objects and *operations* which can be described in terms of the manipulation of equations. Particular systems which figure prominently in algebraic theory are *semigroups*, *groups*, *rings* and *fields*. Several aspects of ordinary arithmetic can be described in terms of these systems. The objects of algebraic systems do not have to be numbers and algebra has been applied in many scientific disciplines. Applications in computing include switching algebra, the relational algebra and algebraic specification of data types. Algebra is more concerned with the results of *operations* than with the constructibility of the objects over which *operations* are defined. Hence algebraic proofs often make implicit assumptions of existence. This must be remembered when using algebraic semantics for programming and formal specification languages.

Algebraic [STh]: A *complete partial order* is algebraic if, for every *element* x, the *set* of *finite elements* y with $y \le x$ forms a *directed set* with *least upper bound* x.

Algebraic System [Alg]. See *algebra*.

Algebra of Regular Expressions [Alg]: a *Boolean algebra* formed by *regular sets* under the *operations* of *union, intersection* and *complement*.

Algorithm [Gen]: means of carrying out a task in a finite number of steps; [Com] a computational procedure which always terminates, e.g. Euclid's algorithm.

Alphabet [Lan]: a *set* of symbols over which *sentences* of a *language* are defined; [Aut]: a *set* of symbols over which input and output *strings* of an *automaton* are defined.

Alternation [Log]: *disjunction*; see *or*.

Alternative Command [PTh]: a composite *guarded command* in which one of a *finite* number of commands is executed if its *guard* is true.

Ambiguous [Lan]: of a *grammar*, possessing a *sentence* with at least two distinct *derivation trees*.

And [Log]: a *logical connective* often denoted by the symbol '&' or '∧' such that if P and Q are *propositions* then the *proposition* P & Q is true if and only if both P and Q are true; otherwise it is false.

Antecedent [Log]: the *proposition* denoted by P in a *propositional formula* of the form $P \Rightarrow Q$.

Antisymmetric [STh]: of a *relation* R, having the property that whenever $<x, y>$ and $<y, x>$ are both in R, then $x = y$.

Application Program Generator [SwT]: a software package used to generate particular types of application program usually without using *imperative* parameters.

Applicative [PTh]: expressed in terms of the application of *functions* to arguments. Cf. *imperative*.

Arc [GNT]: a connection between two *vertices* of a *graph*.

Argument [STh]: an *element* of the *domain* of a *function*.

Articulation Point [GNT]: a *vertex* v of an *undirected connected graph* G is said to be an articulation point if and only if the *graph* resulting when v and all *arcs* involving it are deleted from G is not *connected;* similarly for a *directed graph* G with '*connected*' replaced by '*weakly connected*' throughout.

As-Long-As [Log]: an operator in *temporal logic* such that the assertion A as-long-as B expresses the condition that B is true while A continues to be true.

Assertion Sign [Log]: the sign ⊢ used to mean 'allows the inference that', i.e. such that there is a *derivation* from a *premise* to a *conclusion* (e.g. $P, P \Rightarrow Q$ ⊢ Q).

Assertional Semantics [PTh]: a means of specifying the *semantics* of a programming language by defining the conditions which hold after the execution of a statement given the conditions which hold prior to its execution.

Assignment [PTh]: a programming language construct whose elaboration has the effect of associating a value with a program *variable*.

Assignment Command [PTh]: an elementary *guarded command* which effects an *assignment*.

Associative [Alg]: an *algebraic system* is said to be associative over an *operation* • if, for all *elements* A, B and C in the system, $(A \bullet B) \bullet C = A \bullet (B \bullet C)$.

Assumption [Log]: a *proposition* introduced without *proof* into a *deduction* as a starting point for a *derivation*.

Asynchronous [PPr]: especially of *processes*—progressing independently.

Atom [Com]: an indivisible component (e.g. in a *recursion equation*); [Log]: term occasionally used to refer to a *predicate formula* or part of such a *formula* of the form Fx, Fxy, etc.

Augmented Grammar [Lan]: a *grammar* into which additional *productions* have been introduced in order to facilitate the use of a particular *parsing* strategy. The term may be used rather loosely.

Automaton [Aut]: generic term embracing abstract machines from *finite state machines* through to *Turing machines*, usually described in terms of *states* and *tapes*.

Automorphism [Alg]: an *isomorphism* whose *codomain* is identical to its *domain*.

Axiom (n) [Gen]: a fundamental *assumption* in a *calculus* or *theory* whence *theorems* may be obtained by successive application of the rules of the *calculus* or *theory*; [Log]: a *rule of inference* in the *propositional calculus* or *predicate calculus* which permits a *proposition* to be inferred from no others; [STh]: a rule asserting the existence of *primitive sets* and *sets* obtained by combinations of *primitive sets*.

Axiom Of Choice [STh]: see *Choice, Axiom of*.

Axiom Schema (n) [STh, Log]: a rule which admits all statements of a particular form as *axioms* in *set theory* or *logic*.

B

B-Tree [PPr]: a form of *binary tree* kept nearly symmetric about its *root* for optimal searching and often used in indexing applications.

Backus-Naur Form [Lan]: a notation used in the specification of *syntax*, first used in the report on the Algorithmic Language Algol 60. The *languages* that can be specified by BNF are precisely the *Type 2 languages*.

Backtracking [PPr]: a process of partially 'undoing' steps in a non-deterministic *algorithm* when a wrong step has been taken and alternative steps must be carried out to obtain a solution, used particularly in connection with *parsing*.

Base [Top]: in a *topological space*, a collection ϑ of *open sets* such that every *open set* is the *union* of *elements* of ϑ.

Base Functions [Com]: *functions* in terms of which other *functions* are defined by means of *recursion equations*.

Biconditional [Log]: a *logical connective*, often denoted by the symbol $\Leftrightarrow$; if P and Q are *propositions*, then the *proposition* $P \Leftrightarrow Q$ is true if P and Q are either simultaneously true or simultaneously false, otherwise the *proposition* is false.

Bijective [Alg]: *injective* and *surjective*.

Binary [Gen]: pertaining to two or a pair, e.g. binary *connective*, binary *predicate*, binary *operation*, binary *tree*. Cf. *unary, ternary, n-ary*.

Binary Tree [PPr]: either an *empty tree* or a *node* (the 'root node'), which may contain data, together with two binary trees (the 'left and right subtrees').

Binding Rules [PTh]: *semantic rules* according to which *identifiers* are associated with objects represented in areas of storage in the environment of a program.

Block Structure [PTh]: a feature of programming languages such as Algol 60 and Pascal in which programs are syntactically subdivided into segments called blocks so as to associate *scopes* with *identifiers*.

Bottom-Up Design [PPr]: the process of designing programs by providing common processing elements first and then combining these to form larger components. Cf. *top-down design*.

Bottom-Up Parsing [Lan]: a *parsing* strategy (often used with *LR(K)* grammars) in which a search for a *derivation* is driven by the text to be *parsed*.

Boolean Algebra [Alg]: an *algebraic system* with *operations* + and • satisfying the following rules:

1. $a+a=a \cdot a=a$
2. $a+b=b+a, a \cdot b=b \cdot a$
3. $a+(b+c)=(a+b)+c$
   $a \cdot (b \cdot c)=(a \cdot b) \cdot c$
4. $a \cdot (a+b)=a+(a \cdot b)=a$
5. $a \cdot (b+c)=(a \cdot b)+(a \cdot c)$
   $a+(b \cdot c)=(a+b) \cdot (a+c)$
6. There are universal bounds O and I such that
   $a+O=a, a \cdot O=O, a+I=I, a \cdot I=I$
7. There is a *unary operation* ' such that
   $a \cdot a'=O, a+a'=I$

Bound Variable [Log]: an occurrence of a *variable* in a *predicate formula* which is cited in a *quantifier* and is within the *scope* of that *quantifier*. For example, in $(\forall x)Q(x) \vee P(x)$, the first two occurrences of x are bound and the third occurrence of x unbound.

Boundary Clash [PPr]: absence of *homomorphism* between the inputs and the outputs of a program.

Branching-Time (adj) [Log]: a kind of *interpretation* of *temporal logic* in which many possible futures may follow a given state in time.

C

Calculable [Com]: *computable* or *derivable* in a *calculus*.

Calculus [Gen]: a system of mathematical inference or computation in which results are obtained by the manipulation of formal symbols and expressions according to a *finite set* of precisely defined rules, e.g. the *propositional calculus*; the *calculus of communicating systems*.

Calculus of Communicating Systems [PTh]: a *calculus* for reasoning about communicating systems devised by A.J.R.G. Milner at the University of Edinburgh and usually referred to by the abbreviation *CCS*. An independent element of a communicating system is represented in *CCS* by an *agent*. *Agents* can be combined sequentially, conditionally or in parallel and *scope* rules qualify the interpretation of variables. *Agents* are regarded as *observationally equivalent* if they are indistinguishable in their external communications. *Rules of inference* permit demonstration of *equivalences* whence *equivalence classes* of *agents* may be defined. Such *equivalence classes* are held to be general abstractions of the behaviour of a communicating system. Derived calculi of *CCS* may be defined in terms of primitive notions of *CCS* by means of *rewriting rules*. Differing interpretations of both *CCS* and its derived calculi yield various models for communicating systems.

Cancellation, Laws of [Alg]: laws for *operations* • in *algebraic systems* such that given $a \cdot b = a \cdot c$ or $b \cdot a = c \cdot a$, we may infer that $b = c$.

Canonical (adj) [Gen]: arranged or constructed in a particular standard manner (e.g. *canonical form* of an *expression*).

Canonical Form [Gen]: a way of writing a formal *expression* according to a particular convention.

Canonical System [Com]: a general form of *combinatorial system* possessing in general more than one *axiom*.

Cardinal Number [STh]: the number of *elements* in a *set*.

Cartesian Product [STh]: the Cartesian product of *sets A* and *B* is the *set* of *ordered pairs* (x, y) such that x is in A and y is in B.

Certification [PPr]: the issue of a certificate confirming the results of a test or tests carried out by an independent testing agency to assess compliance of a software product with specified requirements.

Chain (n) [Com]: a *sequence* of *recursive functions, partially ordered* by the *set inclusion relation*; [STh]: a *subset T* of a *set S* with a *partial ordering* $\le$ on S such that $\le$ is a *total ordering* on T.

Channel (n) [PTh]: term adopted from information theory and applied loosely to refer to the means or medium through which communicating entities pass information to each other.

Choice [PTh]: *selection*.

Choice, Axiom of [STh]: an *axiom* required for the proof of certain results involving *infinite sets* which asserts that, for any *set* ϑ of pairwise *disjoint sets*, there is a *set S* which contains exactly one *element* of each *set* in ϑ. Cf. *well-ordering principle* and *Zorn's lemma*.

Chomsky Normal Form [Lan]: a *canonical form* for a *context-free grammar* in which all *productions* are of the form $A \to BC$ or $A \to x$ where A, B and C are *non-terminals* and x is a *terminal*.

Church-Turing Thesis [Com]: a widely accepted hypothesis that only *functions computable* by *Turing machines* are *computable* in the general sense.

Circuit [GNT]: a *path* in a (*directed* or *undirected*) *graph* leading from a *vertex* to itself.

Clause [PTh] : a *polyadic disjunction* of *literals*.

Closed [Alg]: an *algebraic system* is said to be closed over an *operation* • if, for all *elements* A and B in the system, A • B is also in the system; [Top]: a *subset* of a *topological space* is closed if its *complement* is *open*.

Closed Formula [Log]: a *predicate formula* in which all the *variables* are *bound variables*.

Codomain [STh]: see *function*.

Combinatorial System [Com]: an *abstract calculus* comprising a single *axiom*, which is a *word* over a given *alphabet* together with a *finite set* of *productions*.

Communicating Sequential Processes [PTh]: a specification language developed by C.A.R. Hoare at Oxford University, often abbreviated as *CSP*.

Communication Trees [PTh]: a system of interpretation for *CCS* in which the behaviour of an entity is treated as a *partially ordered set* of communications.

Commutative (adj) [Alg]: a commutative *operation* in an *algebraic system* is one such that $A • B = B • A$ for all A and B in the system; an *algebraic system* with a single commutative *operation* is also said to be commutative, e.g. commutative *group*.

Complement (n) [STh]: if *set* A is a *subset* of *set* B, the complement of A in B is the *set* of *elements* of B that are not *elements* of A. Cf. *difference*.

Complementary [GNT]: the complementary *graph* of a *directed graph* G is the *graph* G' with the same *vertices* as G, and such that (u, v) is an *arc* of G' if and only if it is not an *arc* of G. The complementary *graph* of an *undirected graph* G is the *graph* G' with the same *vertices* as G, and such that {u, v} is an *arc* of G' if and only if it is not an *arc* of G.

Complete [Log, Com]: of a *calculus*, possessing a *completeness* property; [GNT]: an *undirected graph* G = (V, A) is said to be complete if and only if {x, y} belongs to A whenever x and y are distinct *elements* of V; a *directed graph* G = (V, A) is said to be complete if and only if either (x, y) or (y, x) belongs to A whenever x and y belong to V.

Complete Lattice [STh]: a *set* S with a *partial ordering* such that any *non-empty subset* of S has a *least upper bound* and a *greatest lower bound*. Cf. *lattice*.

Complete Partial Order [STh]: a *set* S with a *partial ordering* ≤ such that there is a *least element* for ≤ in S and such that every *non-empty directed subset* T of S has a *least upper bound* in T.

Complete Sequential Machine [Aut]: a *Mealy automaton* for which an initial state and a *set* of final states are defined.

Completeness [Log, Com]: a property of a *calculus* or *theory* by virtue of which all instances of a well-defined class or type of result may be derived by application of the *rules* of the calculus or theory; [Log]: of the *propositional calculus*, that property by virtue of which all *tautologies* can be unconditionally inferred by *derivation*; [Log]: of the *predicate calculus*, that property by virtue of which all *valid formulae* can be unconditionally inferred by *derivation*.

Composition [Gen]: the combination of one or more objects according to a defined convention (e.g. composition of *functions*); [STh]: the composition of two *functions* F and G (written $F \cdot G$) is the *set* of *ordered pairs* $<x, z>$ such that $<x, y>$ is in G and $<y, z>$ is in F for some y.

Composition, Law of [Alg]: a generic term for an *operation* in an *algebraic system*.

Computable [Com]: a *function* is said to be computable if and only if there exists a *Turing machine* capable of computing its value for all values of its *arguments* for which it is defined; [Gen]: a *function* is loosely said to be computable if it can be evaluated by some computer.

Computation Rule [Com, PTh]: a rule according to which occurrences of *functionals* are selected for rewriting during the expansion of a *recursion equation*.

Computational Induction [Com]: an *induction* method used to prove properties of *functions* defined by *recursion schemes*.

Concatenation [Alg, Lan]: the *operation* of juxtaposing two *strings* to form a new *string*, often denoted by '.' (e.g. 'abc'.'def' = 'abcdef').

Concatenation Closure [Alg, Lan]: the concatenation closure of a *set S* of *strings* is denoted $S*$ and is defined to be that *set* of *strings* which includes the *empty string*, all *members* of S, all *strings* of the form $A.B$ where A is a *member* of $S*$ and B is a *member* of S, and no other *strings*.

Conclusion [Log]: the result of a *derivation*.

Concrete [Gen]: the opposite of *abstract*.

Concrete Syntax [PTh]: term used to contrast with *abstract syntax*; *syntax* which specifies the *well-formed expressions* of the *language*, and not merely the kinds of *expressions* which occur in the *language*.

Concurrent [PTh]: proceeding at the same time.

Concurrent Composition [PTh]: the *composition* of separate *processes* running concurrently or constructs for specifying such composition in a *specification* or programming language.

Condition Entry [SwT]: part of a *decision table* specifying combinations of conditions under which actions are carried out.

Condition Stub [SwT]: part of a *decision table* listing conditions referred to in the *condition entry*.

Conditional (adj) [Log]: a term used to mean implication but best avoided since it has connotations in other areas of formal methods; (n) [Com]: a *function* from a *tuple* of truth values to a *set* of functions or *functionals*; (adj) [PTh, PPr]: generic term for a construct in a programming language used for selection between alternative actions.

Configuration [Lan]: the current state of an *automaton* together with a description of the contents of each *tape*.

Congruence [Alg]: an *equivalence relation* which *partitions* an *algebraic system*; often used with respect to an *operation* $\cdot$ to imply that, if a is related to b, then $a \cdot c$ is related to $b \cdot c$ and $c \cdot a$ is related to $c \cdot b$ for all c.

Conjunction [Log]: a *propositional formula* of the form $P \& Q$ where P and Q are any other *propositional formulae*. See also *and*.

Conjunctive Canonical Form [Log]: a way of expressing a *propositional formula* as a *polyadic conjunction* of *polyadic disjunctions*, each of whose disjuncts is either an *atom* or the *negation* of an *atom*.

Conjunctive Normal Form [Log]: *conjunctive canonical form*.

Connected [GNT]: of an *undirected graph*, such that any two *vertices* are connected by a *path*; Cf. *strongly connected, weakly connected*; [STh] a *relation* R is connected with respect to a *set A* if and only if, for all distinct x and y in A, either $<x, y>$ is in R or $<y, x>$ is in R (but not both).

Connective, Logical [Log]: a means of *composition* for *propositions*.

Consequent (n) [Log]: the *proposition* denoted by Q in a *propositional formula* of the form $P \Rightarrow Q$.

Conservative (adj) [GNT]: a *Petri net* is said to be conservative if and only if the number of *tokens* in the net is conserved in all *firing sequences*.

Consistent [Log, Com]: of a *calculus* or *theory*, not permitting the *derivation* of results which contradict each other; of the *propositional calculus* and *predicate calculus*, having the property that no *contradiction* can be unconditionally inferred by derivation.

Construction Rules, Wirth's [PPr]: rules due to the Swiss computer scientist N. Wirth whereby a *control structure* for a file-processing program may be derived from a *regular expression* describing the sequence of symbols or record types in the file.

Constructive (adj) [STh, Com]: not assuming the existence of objects whose existence cannot be inferred by *derivation*.

Context-Free Grammar [Lan]: a *type 2 grammar*.

Context-Free Language [Lan]: a *language generated* by a *context-free grammar*.

Context-Sensitive Grammar [Lan]: a *type 1 grammar*.

Context-Sensitive Language [Lan]: a *language generated* by a *context-sensitive grammar*.

Continuation Model [PTh]: an abstract *semantic model* for the *denotational* definition of *imperative* programming languages with unconditional transfers of control.

Continuous [STh]: of a *monotone function F* whose *domain* and *codomain* are *complete partial orders*, the property that, for all *chains C* with *least upper bound l*, $F(l)$ is the *least upper bound* of $F(C)$; [Top] of a *function F* whose *domain A* and *codomain B* are *topological spaces*, the property that, whenever U is *open* in B, then the *inverse image* of U is *open* in A.

Contradiction [Log]: an inherently false *proposition* (e.g. $P \wedge \neg P$).

Contrapositive (n) [Log]: the contrapositive of the *proposition* $P \Rightarrow Q$ is the proposition $\neg Q \Rightarrow \neg P$.

Converse [Log] the converse of the *proposition* $P \Rightarrow Q$ is the *proposition* $Q \Rightarrow P$; [STh] the converse R^c of the *relation R* is the *set* of all *ordered pairs* $<y, x>$ such that $<x, y>$ is in R.

Corollary [Gen, Log] a *theorem derived* immediately or easily from another *theorem*.

Correctness [PTh]: a property of a program with respect to a condition such that the condition is satisfied whenever the program terminates properly. See also *partially correct*; *totally correct*.

Correspondence [STh, Alg]: generally a *relation*, but often used to represent a *bijective function*.

Correspondence Problem [Com]: in a *combinatorial system*, the problem of finding whether there exists a pair of *strings* such that one is *derivable* from the other by repeated applications of the *productions*; many correspondence problems are not *soluble*.

Countable [STh]: of a *set*, *equipollent* to the *set* of *natural numbers* or any *subset* of such a *set*.

Counterdomain [STh]: *range*.

Counterexample [Log]: an *interpretation* of a *formula* in a *calculus* or *theory*, which shows that the *formula* is not a *theorem*.

Critical Path [GNT]: a *path* in a *graph* which minimises or maximises a given *function* of the *set* of *weights* associated with the *arcs* of the *path*.

Cycle [GNT]: a *circuit* in a (*directed* or *undirected*) *graph* with no repeated *arcs*.

D

Data Structure [PPr, PTh]: a collection of items of data organized and accessed in a defined way; a generic kind of organization for such a structure, e.g. *graph, tree*.

Data Type [PPr, PTh]: a *sort* together with a *set* of *operations* over it.

Dead [GNT]: a *transition* is said to be dead in a *marked Petri net* if and only if there is no *firing sequence* which can *enable* it.

Deadlock [GNT]: a condition of a *marked Petri net* in which all *transitions* are *dead*; [PPr]: a state of a system of co-operating *processes* in which no process can proceed.

Decidable [Com]: a *set* of *propositions* is said to be decidable if and only if there exists a *Turing machine* which, given a representation of any *member* of the *set*, can determine in finite time whether or not the *proposition* is true; see also *semi-decidable*.

Decidability [Com]: that property of a *calculus, canonical system* or *theory* by virtue of which there exists an *algorithm* to decide whether or not any one of an identified class of *formulae* possesses a particular property, e.g. that a *propositional formula* is a *tautology*, that a *predicate formula* is *valid*, or that a *sentence* is *generated* by a *grammar*; see also *semi-decidability*.

Decision Table [PPr, SwT]: a means of specifying an *algorithm* or *process* by listing actions, conditions and the combinations of the conditions under which defined combinations of the actions are carried out.

Deduction [Log]: a *derivation* in a logical *calculus*. Cf. *assumption*.

Deduction Rule [Log]: *rule of inference*.

Deduction Theorem [Log]: a *metatheorem* which states that from a *deduction* of the form $P \vdash Q$, it may be inferred that $\vdash P \Rightarrow Q$.

De Morgan's Laws [Log]: *derived rules* of the *propositional calculus* stating that

1. $\neg P \vee \neg Q \Leftrightarrow \neg(P \wedge Q)$
2. $\neg P \wedge \neg Q \Leftrightarrow \neg(P \vee Q)$;

[Alg]: in a *Boolean algebra*, the equations

1. $\neg A + \neg B = \neg(A \cdot B)$
2. $\neg A \cdot \neg B = \neg(A + B)$;

[STh]: for *subsets* A and B of some *set* U, the equations

1. $U - (A \cup B) = (U - A) \cap (U - B)$
2. $U - (A \cap B) = (U - A) \cup (U - B)$

Denotation [PTh]: an object in a *calculus* or *theory* which is denoted by part or all of the text of a *specification* according to the *denotational semantics* defining the meaning of that specification.

Denotational (adj): see *denotation*.

Denotational Semantics [PTh]: a means of specifying the meaning of a *formal language* by defining a *mapping* from the *language* into a *set* of objects constructible in a *theory* or *set* of *expressions* in a *calculus*.

Denumerable [STh]: *countable*; sometimes used to mean *countable* but not *finite*.

Derivation [Gen]: a sequence of steps by means of which a result is obtained; [Log]: a sequence of applications of *rules of inference* leading from a *premise* to a *conclusion*; [Lan]: a sequence of applications of the *productions* of a *grammar* leading from the *start symbol* to some string of *terminals*. Cf. *sentence*.

Derivation Tree [Lan]: a graphical representation of the steps of a *derivation* in the form of a *tree*.

Derived (adj) [Gen]: see *derivation*.

Derived Rule [Log]: a principle of inference which has been *derived* from given *rules of inference*.

Design [PPr]: the process of devising an *implementation* of a *specification*.

Deterministic Grammar [Lan]: a *context-free grammar* where at any stage in any *leftmost derivation* the next *production* to be applied can be determined by examining a *finite* initial *substring* of the unreduced part of the presently obtained *string*.

Deterministic Language [Lan]: a *language* generated by a *deterministic grammar*.

Deterministic Machine [Aut]: an *automaton* in which the next *configuration* is uniquely determined by its present *configuration*.

Difference [STh]: of two *sets* A and B, the *set* whose *members* are exactly those *members* of A which are not in B. The difference of A and B is commonly denoted by $A - B$. Cf. *complement, symmetric difference*.

Direct Proof [Log]: a *deduction* in which a positive *conclusion* is inferred as a result rather than one in which the *negation* of the result is shown to yield a *contradiction*.

Directed Graph [GNT]: see *graph*.

Directed Set [STh]: a *non-empty subset T* of a *set S*, where there is a *partial ordering* $\leq$ on *S*, such that every pair of *elements* in *T* has an *upper bound* in *T*.

Disabled [GNT]: of a *transition* in a *Petri net*, unable to *fire*; [Gen]: of a *process* in a system of co-operating processes (such as an operating system), unable to proceed.

Discharged Assumption [Log]: in an application of a rule such as a rule of conditional proof or *reductio ad absurdum*, the *proposition* which becomes the *antecedent* in the *derived implication*.

Disjoint [STh]: of two *sets A* and *B*, having the property that the *intersection* $A \cap B$ is the *empty set*.

Disjunction [Log]: a *propositional formula* of the form $P \vee Q$ where *P* and *Q* are any other *propositional formulae*. See also *or*.

Disjunctive Canonical Form [Log]: an arrangement of a *propositional formula* as a *polyadic disjunction* of *polyadic conjunctions* each of which is either an *atom* or the *negation* of an atom.

Disjunctive Normal Form [Log]: *disjunctive canonical form*.

Distributed Union [STh]: see *polyadic union*.

Domain [Log]: a class of values whence are chosen particular elements to form an *interpretation* of a *predicate formula*; [STh]: see *function*; also used to denote an *algebraic complete partial order* in which the *set* of *finite elements* is *countable*.

Double Negation, Rule of [Log]: a *rule of inference* allowing *P* to be inferred from $\neg \neg P$. This rule is not included in some systems such as the *intuitionist propositional calculus*.

Dyadic [Gen]: of or pertaining to two, e.g. dyadic *operation* (an *operation* taking two operands), dyadic *predicate* (a predicate applying to two objects). Cf. *monadic, polyadic*.

Dynamic Semantics [PTh]: the *semantics* of a programming language which is concerned with conditions arising only at run time. Cf. *static semantics*.

E

Earley's Algorithm [Lan]: a *parsing* method based on generation of a limited set of alternatives for the *production* to be applied at each stage of a *derivation* and producing a *parse* in cubic time order and quadratic space order according to the length of the *parsed string*.

Edge [GNT]: see *graph*.

Element [STh]: an object belonging to a *set* ; '$x \in A$' signifies that *x* is an element (or *member*) of the *set A*.

Embedding [GNT]: of a *graph* in a space, a *function F* from the *graph* to the space such that every *vertex* of the graph is mapped onto a point of the space, each *arc* of the *graph* joining *vertices u* and *v* onto a line joining $F(u)$ and $F(v)$ in the space, and such that no two lines in the image of the *graph* intersect.

Emptiness Problem [Lan]: the problem of deciding whether the *language* generated by some *grammar* is the *empty set*.

Empty Set [STh]: the *set* which has no *elements*, often denoted by { } or φ.

Empty String [Gen]: the *string* of length 0.

Empty Tree [GNT]: the *tree* with no *vertices* or *arcs*.

Empty Word [Lan]: the *word* corresponding to the *empty string*, often denoted by λ or ε.

Enable [GNT]: see *enabled*

Enabled [GNT]: of a *transition* in a *Petri net*, having *tokens* at each of its *input places*.

Endomorphism [Alg]: a *homomorphism* whose *codomain* is the same as its *domain*.

Environment [PPr]: of a program or *process*, the set of *bindings* in force at any instant during execution.

Epimorphism [Alg]: a *homomorphism* which is *surjective*.

Equality [Gen]: being the same, in number, size, value etc., as.

Equipollent (adj) [STh]: of two *sets A* and *B*, having the same number of *elements*, i.e. such that there is a *bijective function from A to B*.

Equivalence [Log]: that property of two *propositions* whereby they are either both true or both false; [Log]: another term for the *biconditional connective*.

Equivalence Class [STh]: given an *equivalence relation R* on a *set S*, the *set* of *elements* of *S* which are related to a given *element* of *S*.

Equivalence Relation [STh]: a *relation* which is *reflexive*, *symmetric* and *transitive*.

Equivalent [Log]: see *equivalence*.

Event [PPr, PTh]: an occurrence which changes the state of a program or *process*; the *abstraction* of such an occurrence in a *formal model* of such programs or processes.

Eventually [Log]: an operator in *temporal logic*, often denoted by ◇, such that ◇*P* expresses the condition that at some future time *P* will become true.

Excluded Middle, Law of the [Log]: a *derived rule* of the *propositional calculus* which allows the unconditional assertion of *propositions* of the form $P \lor \neg P$. This principle is not derivable in, for example, the *intuitionist propositional calculus*.

Excluded Miracle, Law of the [PTh]: a property of *guarded commands* such that only false *pre-conditions* lead to false *post-conditions*.

Exclusive Or [Log]: a *logical connective*, often denoted by the symbol '$\underline{\vee}$', such that, if *P* and *Q* are *propositions*, then the *proposition* $P \underline{\vee} Q$ is true if and only if precisely one of *P* and *Q* are true; otherwise it is false. Cf. *or*.

Existential Quantifier [Log]: a *quantifier* usually written '∃*x*' and read 'there exists *x*'. Cf. *universal quantifier*.

Expression [Gen]: a written representation of an object or condition in accordance with the *formation rules* of a *calculus* or *theory*.

Extended Entry Decision Table [SwT, PPr]: a *decision table* in which the *condition entry* can contain logical formulae as well as selections given conditions.

Extended Petri Net [GNT]: a *Petri net* augmented by some form of weighting or labelling of its *arcs*, or by inhibiting *input places*.

F

Fairness [PTh]: a property of a system of co-operating *processes* such that no *process* is arbitrarily prevented from or delayed in progressing.

Field [Alg]: a *ring* in which every *element* (except for the *identity element* for the *operation* +) has an *inverse* in the system under •.

Finite [STh]: of a *set*, not *equipollent* to any of its *proper subsets*.

Finite Automaton [Aut]: the simplest form of abstract machine, usually defined as a *5-tuple* (S, I, T, s_1, F) where S is a *non-empty set* of states, I is an *finite* input *alphabet*, T is a *mapping* from $S \times I$ into S, s_1, a *member* of S, is the initial state and F, a *subset* of S, is the *set* of final states.

Finite Control [Aut, Com]: that part of an *automaton* which determines the next move of the machine according to the current *configuration*.

Finite Element [STh]: an *element* x in a *complete partial order* such that whenever $x \leq l$ and l is the *least upper bound* of a *directed subset* T, then $x \leq y$ for some y in T.

Finite State Machine [Aut]: a *Mealy automaton*.

Finite State Model [Aut]: a model based on a *finite state machine*.

Finiteness Problem [Lan]: the problem of deciding whether the *language* generated by a *grammar* is *finite*.

Firable [GNT]: see *firing*.

Fire (v.i.) [GNT]: see *firing*.

Firing [GNT]: in a *Petri net*, the movement of *tokens* from the *input places* of a *transition* to its *output places*.

Firing Sequence [GNT]: a sequence of *firings* of *transitions* in a *Petri net*.

First Order Predicate Calculus [Log]: a *predicate calculus* permitting *quantification* over *individuals* but not over *predicates*.

Fixpoint [Com]: a solution of a *recursion scheme*.

Flow (n) [GNT]: a *traversal* of an object along a *path* in a *graph*; an assignment of *weights* to the *arcs* of a *directed graph*, usually subject to conservation laws at most *vertices*.

Formal Development Method [Gen]: a *formal method* for expressing software *specifications* and undertaking verified *design*.

Formal Description Technique [Gen]: a means of characterising a system based on an abstract model so as to permit reasoning about the system by means of *derivations* in an associated *calculus* or *theory*.

Formal Language [Lan]: a *set* of *strings* over a non-empty *alphabet*.

Formal Method [Gen]: a method making use of a *calculus* or *theory* to analyse or reason about software *specification* and/or *design*.

Formal Model [Gen]: a model defined using *formal methods*.

Formal Specification Language [Gen]: *metalanguage*.

Formation Rules [Log]: in a *calculus*, rules according to which a *formula* is considered to be *well-formed*.

Formula [Gen]: *expression*; [Log] a *sequence* of symbols of a *calculus* which may or may not be *well-formed*.

Free-Choice Net [GNT]: a *Petri net* in which each *arc* from a *place* is either the unique output of that place or the unique input to a *transition*.

Free Variable [Log]: an occurrence of a *variable* in a *predicate formula* which is not within the *scope* of a *quantifier* citing the same *variable*.

Full Graph [GNT]: a *graph* $G = (V, A)$ where $A = V \times V$. Cf. *complete graph*.

Function [STh]: see *function from A to B*.

Function from A to B [STh]: two *sets* A, the *domain*, and B, the *codomain*, together with a *set* G of *ordered pairs* $<x, y>$ where x is an *element* of A and y is an *element* of B, with the property that, for each x in A, there is exactly one y in B such that $<x, y>$ is in G; it is common to write $y = G(x)$. Also referred to as a *total function*. Cf. *partial function*.

Function from A onto B [Alg]: a *surjective function* whose *domain* is A and *codomain* is B.

Functional (n) [STh, Com]: a *function* from a *set* of *functions* into itself.

G

General Recursion Equation [Com]: an equation involving the number zero, the *successor function* over *natural numbers, composition* of *functions* and the *minimisation operator*.

General Recursion Scheme [Com]: a collection of one or more *general recursion equations*.

General Recursive Function [Com]: a *function* satisfying the equations of a *general recursion scheme*.

Generalised Sequential Machine [Aut]: an augmented form of *complete sequential machine* in which the outputs can be strings of any finite length (i.e. the *transition function* maps $S \times I$ into $S \times O^*$, where O^* is the *set of strings* over O).

Generate (v) [Gen]: yield by a procedure, e.g. [Alg] a *set* of *generators* of a *group* is said to generate the *group*, also [Lan] a *grammar* is said to generate a *string* if and only if there exists a *derivation* of that *string* using the *productions* of the *grammar*.

Generator [Alg]: a *set* of *elements* of a *group* such that the *set* of products of the *elements* under the given *operation* constitutes the whole *group*.

Grammar [Lan]: a *combinatorial system* which *generates* a *language* and defined as a 4-*tuple* (V, T, P, S) where V and T are *disjoint*, V is a *set* of *variables* or *non-terminals*, T is a *set* of *terminals*, P is a *set* of *productions*, being a *relation* between *non-empty strings* in $V \cup T$ and *strings* in $V \cup T$, and S is the *start symbol* from which *sentences* are *derived*.

Graph [GNT]: a collection of *vertices* (or *nodes*) and *arcs* (or *lines* or *edges*); formally an *ordered pair* (V, A) where V is a *non-empty set* of *vertices* and A is either a collection of *unordered pairs* of *elements* of V (an *undirected graph*) or a collection of *ordered pairs* of *elements* of V (a *directed graph*); [STh]: the *set* of *ordered pairs* constituting a *function*.

Greatest Element [STh]: of a *set S* with a *partial ordering* ≤, an *element x* such that $y \leq x$ for all y in S.

Greatest Lower Bound [STh]: of a *subset T* of a *set S* with a *partial ordering* ≤, the *greatest element* of the *set* of *lower bounds* for T.

Greibach Normal Form [Lan]: a *canonical form* for a *context-free grammar* in which every *production* is of the form $A \rightarrow aX$, where A is a *non-terminal*, a is a *terminal* and X is a *string of non-terminals*.

Group (n) [Alg]: an *algebraic system* comprising a *set* of *elements* and an *operation* such that the system is *closed* and *associative* with respect to the *operation*, there is an *identity element* in the system and each *element* has an *inverse* in the system.

Guard (n) [PTh]: a condition in a *guarded command*.

Guarded Command [PTh]: a generalised form of program statement devised by E.W. Dijkstra in which the action to be performed is preceded by a condition called a *guard* and such that the action is carried out only if the condition is true.

Guarded Command Language [PTh]: a specification language based on *guarded commands* devised by E.W. Dijkstra and extended by C.A.R. Hoare as a basis for *CSP*.

H

Hausdorff [Top]: of a *topological space*, having the property that, for every pair of distinct *elements x* and x', there are *disjoint open sets U* and U' containing x and x' respectively.

Henceforth [Log]: an operator in *temporal logic*, often denoted by □, such that $\square P$ asserts that P will be true at all future times.

Herbrand Universe [Com]: a *domain* of *interpretation* for a *recursion scheme* whose *elements* are denoted by a *set* of *well-formed expressions* subject to a given *set* of *formation rules*.

Heuristic Method [Gen]: a method based on intuition or empirical methods, e.g. heuristic algorithm.

Homomorphism [Alg]: a *function* from a *set S* with associated *operation* • to a *set S'* with *operation* •′ which 'carries over' the *operation*, i.e. where $f(x \cdot y) = f(x) \cdot' f(y)$ for all x and y in S.

Horn Clause [PTh]: a way of writing a logical expression for use in a logic programming language such as Prolog. A *clause* with at most one *positive literal*.

I

Idempotent [STh]: of a *mapping M* and an *element a*, having the property that $M(a) = a$; [Alg]: of an *operation* • or *element A* of an *algebraic system*, having the property that $A•A = A$.

Identifier [PTh]: a *terminal element* of the *syntax* of a programming language which denotes some object according to the *binding rules* of the language.

Identity [Log, STh]: *equality* between objects; [Alg]: an *element* in an *algebraic system* which is both a *left identity* and a *right identity element*.

Identity Relation [STh]: on a given *set*, the *relation* consisting of all *ordered pairs* of the form $<x, x>$.

Image [Alg]: the *range* of a *function* or *morphism*.

Imperative (adj) [PTh]: specifying, requesting or expressed in terms of action, e.g. imperative programming language. Cf. *applicative*.

Implementation [PPr]: the realisation of a system which is the subject of a *specification*, especially of software systems.

Implication [Log]: a *logical connective*, often denoted by the symbol '$\Rightarrow$', such that if *P* and *Q* are *propositions*, then the *proposition* $P \Rightarrow Q$ is false if and only if *P* is true and *Q* is false.

Includes [STh] see *inclusion*.

Inclusion [STh]: a *relation* on *sets*, where '*A includes B*' if and only if *B* is a *subset* of *A*.

Inconsistency [Log, Com]: see *inconsistent*.

Inconsistent [Log, Com]: of a *calculus* or *theory*, permitting the *derivation* of results which contradict each other; of a logical *calculus*, having the property that a *contradiction* can be unconditionally inferred by *derivation*.

Individual (n) [Log]: an object of which a *predicate* may be true or false; [STh]: an object which is not a *set*.

Induction [STh, Com]: a method of *proof*, very common in computation theory, whereby a *proposition* is proved true for a particular *member* of a *set*, it is further proved that truth for an arbitrary *member* implies truth for certain other *members* and then, subject to suitable other *premises*, inferred that in consequence the *proposition* is true for all *members* of the *set*.

Inductive Assertion [PTh]: an assertion about the *environment* of a program which is true for all possible instances of that *environment*.

Inference, Rule of [Log]: see *rule of inference*.

Infinite [STh]: of a *set*, not *finite*. See also *countable* and *uncountable*.

Infinity, Axiom of [STh]: an *axiom* of certain formulations of *set theory* asserting the existence of *infinite sets*.

Infix Notation [PPr, PTh]: a way of writing *expressions* such that *operators* occur between the operands to which they refer.

Inherent Ambiguity [Lan]: a property of a *language* such that all *grammars* which *generate* it are *ambiguous*.

Initial Algebra [Alg]: the minimal *algebraic system* satisfying a collection of abstract algebraic equations.

Injective [STh]: of a *function*, such that no two distinct *elements* of the *domain* map to a single *element* of the *range*, in other words such that $f(x) = f(y)$ implies $x = y$.

Input Place [GNT]: a *place* in a *Petri net* to which no *arc* leads; of a *transition*, a place from which the *firing* of that *transition* conveys a *token*.

Interderivable [Log]: of *propositions*, derivable from each other; propositions P and Q are interderivable if and only if $P \vdash Q$ and $Q \vdash P$.

Internal Event [Gen, Aut, PTh] any *event* in a system which is not externally observable.

Interpretation [Log, STh]: an assignment of values to the *variables* of an *expression* in a *calculus* or *theory* in order to obtain a value for the *expression*.

Intersection [STh]: of two *sets A* and *B*, the *set* whose *members* are exactly those in both *A* and *B*. The intersection of *A* and *B* is commonly denoted by $A \cap B$. More generally, the intersection of any *set* ϑ of *sets* consists of those *elements* lying in all of the *sets* in ϑ; see *polyadic intersection*.

Intuitionism [Log]: a school of thought among logicians which, among other things, denies the validity of the rule of *double negation* as a *rule of inference*.

Intuitionist [Log]: see *intuitionism*.

Invariant [Alg]: a property of an *algebraic system* which is preserved under a *morphism*; also see *loop invariant*.

Inverse (n) [STh]: of a *function* (considered as a *relation*), the *converse* of the *relation*; [Alg] for an *element A* in an *algebraic system* with *operation* •, the *element A'* such that $A \cdot A' = A' \cdot A = I$ where I is the *identity element*.

Inverse Image [STh]: of a *subset T* of the *codomain* of a *function F*, the *set* of all x in the *domain* of F such that $F(x)$ is an *element* of T.

Inverse Production [Com]: in a *combinatorial system*, the inverse of the *production* $\alpha \to \beta$ is the *production* $\beta \to \alpha$.

Irreflexive [STh]: of a *relation R*, having the property that no *ordered pair* $<x, x>$ is in R.

Isomorphism [Alg]: a *homomorphism* which is *bijective*.

J

Jackson Structured Programming [PPr]: a methodology for *structured programming* based on *construction rules* due to N. Wirth, elaborated for use in commercial data-processing by M. A. Jackson and taught by his organisation as a proprietary technique.

Jackson System Development [PPr]: an extension of *Jackson Structured Programming*, applied to systems rather than simply to programs, developed by M. A. Jackson and taught by his organisation as a proprietary methodology.

K

***k*-Bounded** [GNT]: of a *Petri net*, having at most *k tokens* in any one *place* for all *markings* in the *reachability set*.

Kernel [Alg]: the *set* of *elements* of an *algebraic system G* which are mapped onto the *identity element* of a system *G'* under a *homomorphism*.

L

Labelled Petri Net [GNT]: a *Petri net* in which an object called a 'label' is associated with each *arc* in the net.

Language [Gen]: a collection of *expressions* complying with specified requirements; [Lan]: a *set* of *strings*, especially as *generated* by a *grammar*.

Language of Temporal Ordering Specification (LOTOS) [PTh]: a *formal specification language* developed at the University of Twente for specifying *OSI services* and *protocols*.

Lattice [STh]: a *set S* with a *partial ordering* such that any *non-empty finite subset* of *S* has a *least upper bound* and a *greatest lower bound*; [Alg]: an *algebraic system* with *operations* + and • which is *idempotent, commutative, associative* and satisfies the *property of absorption*, such as *Boolean algebra*.

Lazy Evaluation [PPr]: a method of evaluating an *expression* in which execution of *operations* is deferred until the result is required.

Leaf [GNT]: a *node* in a *directed tree* from which no *arc* leads.

Least Element [STh]: of a *set S* with a *partial ordering* ≤, an *element x* such that $x \le y$ for all y in *S*.

Least Upper Bound [STh]: of a *subset T* of a *set S* with a *partial ordering* ≤, the *least element* of the *set* of *upper bounds* for *T*; [Com] where the *set* in question is a *set of fixpoints* of a *recursion scheme* ordered by a *chain*.

Left Identity [Alg]: an *element e* in an *algebraic system* is a left identity with respect to an *operation* • if $e \cdot x = x$ for every *element x* of the system.

Leftmost Derivation [Lan]: a *derivation* in a *context-free grammar* in which at each step the leftmost *non-terminal* of a *sentential form* is the subject of the next *production* to be applied.

Lexeme [Lan]: a *substring* of a *string* determined by *lexical analysis*.

Lexical Analysis [Lan]: the segmentation of a *string* (such as source code of a program) into distinct *substrings* (such as identifiers, operators, etc.) which are treated as indivisible units for the purpose of *syntax analysis*.

Limited Entry Decision Table [SwT]: a form of *decision table* in which only two-valued entries, such as true/false or selected/not selected, are allowed in the *condition entries* and *action entries*. Cf. *extended entry decision table*.

Linear Bounded Automaton [Com , Lan]: a *non-deterministic Turing machine* which never scans any part of its *tape* outside that portion on which its input is written. The class of such machines recognizes the class of *context-sensitive languages*.

Linear Grammar [Lan]: a *grammar* whose *productions* are all of the form $A \rightarrow xBy$ or $A \rightarrow x$, where A and B are *non-terminals* and x and y are *strings* of *terminals*.

Linear Language [Lan]: a *language generated* by a *linear grammar*.

Linear-Time Model [Log]: a system of interpretation for *temporal logic* in which only one future can follow a given history.

List (n) [PPr]: a *data structure* in which each item is accompanied by a reference to another for the purposes of grouping or ordering.

Literal (n) [PTh]: a *lexeme* whose *denotation* is independent of the *environment* of a program or *process*; [Log]: an *atom* (a *positive literal*) or the *negation* of an *atom* (a *negative literal*).

Live (adj) [GNT]: of a *transition* in a *Petri net*, potentially *firable* in all *reachable markings*.

Livelock [GNT, PPr]: a condition of a system of co-operating *processes* which is not *deadlock* but in which no useful processing is being done and from which no exit can be effected.

Liveness [GNT]: the property of being *live*.

LL(K) Grammar [Lan]: a *grammar* such that from a *leftmost derivation* of a *sentential form* xAX, where x is a *string* of *terminals*, A is a *non-terminal* and X is an unreduced *sentential form*, at most the next K input symbols determine the *production* to be used to reduce A.

LL(K) Language [Lan]: a *language generated* by an *LL(K) grammar*.

Logic [Gen]: those branches of mathematics and philosophy dealing with reasoning and inference.

Logical Connective [Log]: see *connective, logical*.

Lookahead (n) [Lan]: a technique used to determine which *production* to apply next in *parsing* a *string* according to a *deterministic grammar*.

Loop [GNT]: in a *graph*, an *arc* from a *vertex* to itself.

Loop Invariant [PTh]: an *inductive assertion* which is true throughout the execution of a loop.

Lower Bound [STh]: of a *subset* T of a *set* S with a *partial ordering* $\leq$, an *element* x of S such that $x \leq y$ for all y in S.

LR(K) Grammar [Lan]: a *grammar* such that from a *rightmost derivation* of a *sentential form* XYz, where X and Y are sentential forms containing *non-terminals* and z is a *string* of *terminals*, at most the next K input symbols determine the next *production* to be used.

LR(K) Language [Lan]: a *language generated* by an *LR(K) grammar*.

M

***M*-Complete** [Log]: in *temporal logic*, *complete* under all *interpretations* in a model *M*.

***M*-Consistent** [Log]: in *temporal logic*, *consistent* under all *interpretations* in a model M.

***M*-Equivalent** [Log]: of two *assertions* in *temporal logic*, *equivalent* under all *interpretations* in a model *M*.

***M*-Valid** [Log]: of an assertion in *temporal logic*, *valid* under all *interpretations* in a model *M*.

Many-to-One Relation (n) [STh]: a *relation* such that for at least one *y* there is more than one *x* such that <*x, y*> is in the *relation*.

Map (n) [PTh]: a construct corresponding to a *mapping* in *VDM-SL*.

Mapping (n) [Alg]: various uses, including *relation, partial function* and *function*.

Mapping from *A* to *B* [Alg]: a *function* whose *domain* is a *subset* of *A* and *range* is a *subset* of *B*. Cf. *partial function*.

Marked Petri Net [GNT]: a *Petri net* having exactly one input *transition* and exactly one output *transition* in each *place*.

Marking (n) [GNT]: an allocation of *tokens* to the *places* of a *Petri net*.

Matching Offer [PTh]: in *LOTOS*, the *abstraction* of communication between *processes*.

Matrix [Log]: the part of a *predicate formula* in a *prenex canonical form* which follows the leading *quantifiers*.

Maximal Element [STh]: of a *set S* with a *partial ordering* ≤, an *element x* such that, if $y \in S$ and $x \leq y$, then $x = y$.

Mealy Automaton [Aut]: an augmented form of *finite automaton* capable of outputting *strings* definable as a 4-*tuple* (*S, I, O, T*) where *S* is a *non-empty set* of states, *I* and *O* are respectively *finite* input and output *alphabets* and *T* is the *transition function*. Cf. *generalised sequential machine*.

Meaning Function [PTh]: a *function* in a *semantic metalanguage* which maps a programming language construct into its *denotation*.

Member [STh]: an object belonging to a *set* ; '$x \in A$' signifies that *x* is a member (or *element*) of the *set A*.

Metalanguage [Gen]: a *language* in which another *language* is defined; [PTh] a *language* used to specify systems which may be implemented in a programming language.

Metatheorem [Gen]: a *theorem* of a *metatheory*.

Metatheory [Gen]: a *theory* which deals with the properties of another *theory*.

Minimal Element [STh]: of a *set S* with a *partial ordering* ≤, an *element x* such that, if $y \in S$ and $y \leq x$, then $x = y$.

Minimisation Operator [Com]: an operator on a *function* which selects the least *argument* for which the *function value* satisfies a specified condition; more specifically, if *F* is a *function* with *m arguments* $x_1, x_2, ... , x_m$ which are *natural numbers*, then the minimisation of *F* is the *partial function G* with m-1 *arguments* $x_1, x_2, \ldots, x_{m-1}$ such that $G(x_1, x_2, \ldots, x_{m-1})$ is the least value of k such that $F(x_1, x_2, \ldots, x_{m-1}, k)$ equals *zero*.

Modal Logic [Log]: a branch of *logic* dealing with reasoning proceeding from *assertions* expressed using modal auxiliary verbs.

Modus Ponendo Ponens [Log]: the *rule of inference* which permits the argument $P, P \Rightarrow Q \vdash Q$.

Modus Ponendo Tollens [Log]: the *derived rule* which permits the argument $\neg(P \wedge Q), P \vdash \neg Q$.

Modus Ponens [Log]: *modus ponendo ponens*.

Modus Tollendo Ponens [Log]: the *derived rule* which permits the argument $P \vee Q, \neg P \vdash Q$.

Modus Tollendo Tollens [Log]: the *rule of inference* which permits the argument $P \Rightarrow Q, \neg Q \vdash \neg P$.

Modus Tollens [Log]: *modus tollendo tollens*.

Monadic [Gen]: of or pertaining to one, e.g. monadic operator (an operator taking one operand), monadic *predicate* (a predicate applying to one object). Cf. *dyadic, polyadic*.

Monadic First Order Predicate Calculus [Log]: a form of *first order predicate calculus* in which all *predicates* are *monadic*. *Quantification* is restricted to be over *individuals* rather than over individuals and predicates and for which it is *decidable* whether any *predicate formula* is *valid*.

Monoid (n) [Alg]: a *semigroup* which has an *identity element*.

Monomorphism [Alg]: a *homomorphism* which is *injective*.

Monotone [STh]: of a *function* F with *partial orders* $\leq$ and $\sqsubseteq$ on its *domain* and *codomain* respectively, such that, whenever $x \leq y$, then $F(x) \sqsubseteq F(y)$.

Monotonically Decreasing [STh]: of a *sequence* of values from an *ordered set*, such that each value equals or exceeds those which succeed it in the *sequence*.

Monotonically Increasing [STh]: of a *sequence* of values from an *ordered set*, such that each value equals or exceeds those which precede it in the *sequence*.

Monotonicity [STh]: the property of being either *monotonically increasing* or *monotonically decreasing*.

Moore Automaton [Aut]: the simplest kind of augmented *finite automaton* capable of outputting *strings* and definable as a *5-tuple* (S, I, O, T_1, T_2) where S is a *non-empty set* of states, I and O are *finite* input and output *alphabets* respectively, T_1 is the 'output' *function* mapping S into O and T_2 is the 'transition' *function* mapping $S \times I$ into S. Cf. *complete sequential machine*.

Morphism [Alg]: a *mapping* between *algebraic systems*, especially with an associated *invariant*, e.g. *homomorphism, isomorphism*.

N

n-ary (adj) [Gen]: pertaining to *n*, where *n* is a *natural number*, e.g. *n*-ary *operation*, *n*-ary *relation*. Cf. *unary, binary, ternary*.

n-Tuple (n) [STh]: a *tuple* with *n elements*. Thus, for example, an *ordered pair* is a 2-tuple.

Natural Deduction [Log]: the process of *proof* by *deduction*, especially contrasting with *proof* by *truth valuation*; a natural deduction system has *rules of inference* for each of its *logical connectives*, but no *propositions* deemed to be true a priori.

Natural Number [Gen]: a non-negative whole number.

Necessary Condition [Log]: *P* is a necessary condition for *Q* if and only if $Q \Rightarrow P$.

Negative Literal [PTh] : see *literal*.

Negation (n) [Log]: application of the *'not'* connective.

Net Theory [Gen]: a discipline combining elements of *graph* theory and *automata* theory often used in the characterisation of *concurrent* systems.

Network [Gen]: a collection of connected, communicating systems; [GNT] a *graph* with associated *flows*.

Node [GNT]: see *vertex*.

Noetherian Induction [Gen]: a form of *induction* applied to *partially ordered sets*, sometimes loosely called *structural induction*.

Non-Deterministic Machine [Aut]: an *automaton* in which the next *configuration* may not be uniquely determined by the current configuration.

Non-Empty [STh]: of a *set*, not being *equal* to the *empty set*.

Non-Terminal [Lan]: see *grammar*.

Normal Form [Lan]: *canonical form*.

Normal Production [Com]: a *production* in a *combinatorial system* of the form $xAyBz \Rightarrow x'Ay'Bz'$.

Normal System [Com]: a *combinatorial system* whose *productions* are all *normal productions*.

Not [Log]: a *logical connective* often denoted by the symbol '¬' such that if *P* is a *proposition* then the *proposition* ¬*P* is true if *P* is false, and false if *P* is true.

O

Observational Equivalence [PTh]: of two *agents* in *CCS*, the property of being indistinguishable in terms of their exhibited behaviour.

One-To-One (adj) [Alg]: *injective*.

Onto (adj) [Alg]: *surjective*.

Open Set [Top]: see *topological space*.

Operation [Alg]: on a *set S*, a *function* from *n-tuples* of *elements* of *S* to *S* for some value of *n*; more generally, on a *set ϑ* of *sets*, a *function* from *n-tuples* to some *S* in *ϑ*, where each component in the *n-tuple* belongs to some specified *member* of *ϑ*; see *polyadic operation*.

Operational Semantics [PTh]: a means of specifying the meaning of a programming language by specifying the effect at run time of statement execution.

Operator [Alg]: a *denotation* of an *operation*.

Operator Grammar [Lan]: a *grammar* in which no *production* reduces a *non-terminal* to a form containing two adjacent *non-terminals*.

Operator Language [Lan]: a *language generated* by an *operator grammar*.

Operator Precedence Grammar [Lan]: an *operator grammar* for which an *ordering relation* over its *terminals* provides the basis for selection of *productions* in a deterministic *parsing algorithm*.

Operator Precedence Language [Lan]: a *language generated* by an *operator precedence grammar*.

Or [Log]: a *logical connective*, often denoted by the symbol '∨', such that if, *P* and *Q* are *propositions*, then the *proposition P ∨ Q* is false if and only if both *P* and *Q* are false; otherwise it is true. Cf. *exclusive or*.

Order (n) [Alg]: of an *algebraic system* (such as a *group*), the number of its *elements*; of an *element* of a *group*, the least positive number *k* such that the *k*th power of the *element* is the *identity element* of the system.

Ordered [STh]: see *ordering*.

Ordered Pair [STh] a *set* of the form $\{x, \{x,y\}\}$, often written (x, y) or $<x, y>$. Ordered pairs have the property that $<x, y> = <u, v> \Leftrightarrow x = u$ and $y = v$.

Ordering (n) [STh]: a generic term for a *relation* such as one of the following: a *quasi-ordering*, a *partial ordering*, a *simple ordering*, a *strict partial ordering*, a *strict simple ordering*, a *total ordering* or a *well-ordering*.

Ordering Relation [STh]: *ordering*.

Oriented Graph [GNT]: a *directed graph*.

Output Place [GNT]: a *place* in a *Petri net* from which no *arc* leads; of a *transition*, a *place* to which the *firing* of that *transition* conveys a *token*.

P

Paradox [Gen, Log]: a *contradiction* or other apparently unsound result arrived at either by means of faulty reasoning or as a result of *inconsistency* in a *calculus* or *theory*.

Parallel Command [PTh]: in a *guarded command language*, a construct for *parallel composition*.

Parallel Composition [PPr, PTh]: *composition* of actions such that they can proceed simultaneously.

Parenthesis-Free Notation [PPr, PTh]: *postfix notation* or *prefix notation*.

Parse (n) [Lan]: a sequence of *productions* whose application constitutes a *derivation* of a *string* in a given *language*; (v.t.) [Lan] to produce a *parse*.

Parse Tree [Lan]: *derivation tree*.

Parser [Lan]: a real or abstract *parsing* mechanism.

Parser Generator [SwT]: a software tool generating a *parser* from a given *grammar*, usually of prescribed type such as an *LL(K) grammar* or an *LR(K) grammar*.

Parsing [Lan]: see *parse*.

Partial Function [STh]: two *sets A* and *B*, together with a *set G* of *ordered pairs* <x, y>, where *x* is an *element* of *A* and *y* is an *element* of *B*, with the property that, for each *x* in *A*, there is at most one *y* in *B* such that <x, y> is in *G*. Cf. *total function* and *function*.

Partial Graph [GNT]: a *graph* $G_1 = (V_1, A_1)$ is a partial graph of *graph* $G_2 = (V_2, A_2)$ if and only if $V_1 = V_2$ and A_1 is a *subset* of A_2. Cf. *subgraph*.

Partially Correct [PTh]: of a program with respect to an *inductive assertion*, such that the assertion is true whenever the program terminates.

Partially Ordered [STh]: of a *set*, possessing a *partial ordering*.

Partial Ordering (n) [STh]: a *relation* which is *reflexive, antisymmetric* and *transitive*.

Partial Recursive Function [Com]: a *general recursive function* which may not be defined for all values of its arguments. Cf. *total recursive function*.

Partition (n) [STh]: of a given *set*, a *set* of mutually *disjoint sets* whose *union* is the given *set*; (v.t.) [STh]: to form a partition of.

Path [GNT]: in a *graph*, a *sequence* of *arcs* leading from one *vertex* to another. More formally, in a *directed graph G*, a *sequence* of *vertices* $v_0, v_1, ... , v_n$ such that $\{v_i, v_{i+1}\}$ is an *arc* in *G*; in an *undirected graph G*, a *sequence* of *vertices* $v_0, v_1, ... , v_n$ such that (v_i, v_{i+1}) is an *arc* in *G*.

Path Expression [PTh]: an expression, resembling a *regular expression*, specifying permitted sequences of interaction of resources and *processes*.

Peano's Axioms [Alg]: a system of *axioms* which characterise the system of *natural numbers* thus:

1. *zero* is a *natural number*;
2. the *successor* of a *natural number* is a *natural number*;
3. no *natural number* has *zero* as its *successor*;
4. no two distinct *natural numbers* have the same *successor*; and
5. any *subset* of the *set* of *natural numbers* containing *zero* and also having property (2) is itself the entire *set* of *natural numbers*.

Petri Net [GNT]: a specialised form of *graph* originally defined as a 4-*tuple* (P, T, I, O), where *P* is a *finite set* of *places*, *T* a finite *set* of *transitions* and *I* and *O* are *mappings* from *T* into the *powerset* of *P*. Note that many variants and extensions of this definition are now used.

Petri-Net Language [GNT]: a *language* comprising the *set* of *sequences* of labels corresponding to the *firing sequences* of a *labelled Petri net*.

Phrase Structure Grammar [Lan]: a *grammar* in which a *finite set* of rules defines the way in which a *string* is composed from its *substrings*. The term is used to contrast with rhetorical forms of grammatical specification.

Place (n) [GNT]: a *vertex* of a *Petri net* which may hold one or more *tokens*.

Place-Transition Net [GNT]: *Petri net*.

Planar [GNT]: of a *graph*, representable on flat paper such that no two *arcs* cross each other, i.e. a *graph* with an *embedding* in the plane.

Point (n) [STh]: *element*; [GNT]: *vertex*.

Polish Notation: [PPr, PTh]: *parenthesis-free notation*.

Polish Postfix Notation: [PPr, PTh]: *postfix notation*.

Polish Prefix Notation: [PPr, PTh]: *prefix notation*.

Polyadic [Gen]: of or pertaining to many, e.g. polyadic *operation* (an *operation* with many operands), polyadic *predicate* (a predicate applying to many objects). Cf. *monadic, dyadic*.

Polyadic Conjunction [STh]: the extension of the concept of *conjunction* to many *formulae*.

Polyadic Disjunction [STh]: the extension of the concept of *disjunction* to many *formulae*

Polyadic Intersection [STh]: the extension of the concept of *intersection* to many *sets*.

Polyadic Union [STh]: the extension of the concept of *union* to many *sets*.

Poset [STh]: *partially ordered set*.

Positive Literal [PTh] : see *literal*.

Post-Condition [PTh]: a condition which is asserted to hold after the execution of a program statement.

Post System [Com]: a *combinatorial system* whose *productions* consist of a *set* of *normal productions* and their *inverses*.

Postfix Notation [PPr, PTh]: a way of writing *expressions* such that *operators* follow the operands to which they refer.

Potentially Firable [GNT]: of a *transition* in a *Petri net*, such that there is some *firing sequence* which can *enable* it.

Powerset [STh]: of a *set*, the *set* of all its *subsets*.

Pre-Condition [PTh]: a condition which, if true before the execution of a program statement, should guarantee that the *post-condition* will hold afterwards.

Precedence [Lan]: an *ordering relation* over the *terminals* of a *grammar*; [PPr]: the order of priority in which *operations* are carried out.

Predicate [Log]: a condition which may be true or false of an object or collection of objects; [Log]: the *abstraction* of such a condition in a *calculus*.

Predicate Calculus [Log]: a *calculus* permitting inference involving statements concerning objects and *predicates* which refer to them and for which the truth or falsity of a statement depends on the individuals and predicates involved, e.g. *first order predicate calculus, monadic first order predicate calculus, second order predicate calculus*.

Predicate Formula [Log]: a *sequence* of symbols which is *well-formed* according to the *formation rules* of a *predicate calculus*.

Predicate Transformer [PTh]: an abstract concept of a *process* due to E.W. Dijkstra which views it as transforming a *pre-condition* into a *post-condition*.

Prefix Notation [PPr, PTh]: a way of writing *expressions* such that *operators* precede the operands to which they refer.

Premise [Log]: an *assumption* on which a *conclusion* depends.

Prenex Canonical Form [Log]: an arrangement of a *predicate formula* in which all *quantifiers* are at the beginning.

Prenex Conjunctive Canonical Form [Log]: an arrangement of a *predicate formula* in which all *quantifiers* are at the beginning and the remainder is in *conjunctive canonical form*.

Prenex Conjunctive Normal Form [Log]: *prenex conjunctive canonical form*.

Prenex Disjunctive Canonical Form [Log]: an arrangement of a *predicate formula* in which all *quantifiers* are at the beginning and the remainder is in *disjunctive canonical form*.

Prenex Disjunctive Normal Form [Log]: *prenex disjunctive canonical form*.

Prenex Normal Form [Log]: *prenex canonical form*.

Preordering [Alg]: *quasi-ordering*.

Primitive (adj): given, irreducible or irreplaceable, especially of *axioms* or objects in a *calculus* or *theory*.

Primitive Recursion Equation [Com]: an equation involving only the *atom zero*, the *successor function* over *natural numbers* and *compositions* of *functions*.

Primitive Recursive Function [Com]: a *function* satisfying a *primitive recursion equation*.

Procedural [PTh]: *imperative*.

Process (n) [PPr, PTh]: an entity carrying out processing, especially in co-operation with other similar entities.

Production [Com]: in a *combinatorial system*, and also specifically [Lan] in a *grammar*, a rule of the form $S_1 \rightarrow S_2$, where S_1 and S_2 are *strings*, and stipulating that S_2 may be written in place of S_1 wherever S_1 occurs.

Program Proving [PTh]: *program verification*.

Program Verification [PTh]: the determination of the *correctness* of a program with respect to a specification, i.e. whether it correctly implements the specification.

Proof [Log]: *derivation*.

Proper Subset [STh]: a *subset* of a given *set* which is not the same as the given *set*.

Property of Absorption [Alg]: see *Absorption, Property of*.

Proposition [Gen]: a statement expressing a condition which is either true or false; [Log] the abstraction of such a statement in a *calculus*.

Propositional Calculus [Log]: the *calculus* dealing with inference involving statements considered to be true or false without reference to their form or content.

Propositional Formula [Log]: a sequence of symbols which is *well-formed* according to the *formation rules* of the *propositional calculus*.

Protocol [PPr]: a defined procedure for sustained communication between *processes*.

Pushdown Automaton [Aut, Lan]: an augmented, possibly *non-deterministic, finite automaton* with a last-in-first-out store and where the *transitions* and *operations* on the store depend on the current state, the most recently inserted item in the store and the current input symbol. The class of *languages* recognizable by such *automata* is the class of *context-free languages*.

Q

Quantification [Log]: the use or application of a *quantifier*.
Quantifier [Log]: a *universal quantifier* or an *existential quantifier*.
Quasi-Ordering (n) [STh]: on a *set*, a *reflexive transitive relation*.
Quotient Set [STh]: given an *equivalence relation R* on a *set S*, the *set* of all *equivalence classes* for *R*, often denoted by *S/R*.

R

Range (n) [STh]: of a *function R*, the *set* of all elements *y* such that there exists *x* where (*x*, *y*) is in *R*. (Note that range is sometimes used to denote the *codomain* rather than a *subset* of the *codomain* as here.)
Reachability Set [GNT]: the *set* of *markings* of a *Petri net* which may be reached from an initial marking by a *firing sequence*.
Reachable [GNT]: of a *marking* of a *Petri net,* able to be reached from an initial marking by a *firing sequence*.
Recogniser [Lan]: an abstract machine or procedure which accepts *strings* in a given *language* by entering a final state or outputting a particular symbol.
Recursion Equation [Com]: an equation defining a *function* in which the *function* may appear on both sides of the equation.
Recursion Induction [Com]: an *induction* method for proving properties of *recursion schemes*.
Recursion Scheme [Com]: a collection of one or more *recursion equations*.
Recursion Theorem [Com]: a result stating that, subject to certain *preconditions*, a *recursion scheme* always has a unique least *fixpoint*.
Recursive Definition [Gen]: a definition of which the object being defined forms part, e.g. the definition of *binary tree* in this glossary.
Recursive Function [Com]: a *function* defined by a *general recursion equation*; or, equivalently, a *function computable* by a *Turing Machine*.
Recursive Language [Lan]: a *language* whose *sentences* can be recognized or *generated* by an *algorithm*; more specifically, a *language* that is a *recursive set*.
Recursively Enumerable [Com]: of a *set*, such that there exists a *Turing machine* which can generate the *elements* of the *set* in some order.
Recursive Set [Com]: a *set* such that there exists a *Turing machine* which terminates on all inputs and which decides whether or not a given input represents an *element* of the *set*.

Reducible [Com]: one decision problem is said to be reducible to another if and only if the *decidability* of the first problem implies the *decidability* of the latter.

Reductio Ad Absurdum [Log]: the *rule of inference* which permits the argument $P \Rightarrow Q, P \Rightarrow \neg Q \vdash \neg P$.

Reduction [Lan]: the elimination or replacement of a *substring* of a *sentential form* by application of a *production*.

Reflexive [STh]: of a *relation R* between a *set S* and itself, having the property that $<x, x>$ is in R for all x in S.

Regular Expression [Aut , Lan]: an *expression* over an *alphabet A* according to the following formation rules:

1. φ (the *empty set*) and λ (the *empty word*) are regular expressions;
2. x is a regular expression for any x in A;
3.   if A and B are regular expressions then so are A • B, A + B, A* and B*; and
4.   there are no regular expressions other than those provided by (1), (2) and (3).

Regular Grammar [Lan]: *type 3 grammar*.

Regular Language [Aut, Lan]: a *language generated* by a *regular grammar*.

Regular Set [Aut, Lan]: a *set* denoted by a *regular expression* over an *alphabet A* as follows:

1. $[\varphi]$ = the *empty set*.
2. $[\lambda]$ = the *singleton set* containing the *empty word* λ.
3. $[x] = \{'x'\}$ for each x in A.
4. $[A \cdot B] = [A] \cdot [B]$ (*string concatenation*)
5. $[A + B] = [A] \cup [B]$ (*set union*)
6. $[A^*] = [A]^*$ (*concatenation closure*).

Relabelling [PTh]: changing a formal *expression* to avoid unwanted clashes of *variables* or *identifiers*, especially in *CCS*.

Relation [STh]: usually a relation between *sets A* and *B* is a *set* of *ordered pairs* $<a, b>$ with a in A and b in B; more generally, a *set* of *tuples*.

Rendezvous [PPr]: a point in the evolution of two or more *processes* at which they are all mutually *synchronised*.

Resolution Method [Log]: a procedure for testing whether a *predicate formula* is *valid* by attempting to show that its *negation* is not *satisfiable*.

Rewriting Rule: a *production*, in the generic sense.

Right Identity [Alg]: an *element e* in an *algebraic system* is a right identity with respect to an *operation* • if $x \cdot e = x$ for every *element x* of the system.

Rightmost Derivation [Lan]: a *derivation* in a *grammar* in which at each step the rightmost *non-terminal* of a *sentential form* is the subject of the next *production* to be applied.

Ring (n) [Alg]: an *algebraic system* with *operations* + and • such that it is an *abelian group* with respect to the *operation* +, a *semigroup* with respect to the *operation* •, and the *operation* • is distributive over the *operation* + (i.e. $a \cdot (b + c) = a \cdot b + a \cdot c$ and $(b + c) \cdot a = b \cdot a + b \cdot c$) for all a, b and c.

Root [GNT]: the unique *node* in a *directed tree* to which no *arc* leads.

Rule [SwT]: in a *decision table*, the combination of a *condition entry* and its corresponding *action entry* which specify a discrete element of processing.

Rule Combination [SwT]: for *decision tables*, a method of *rule elimination* based on the identification of *equivalent* rules.

Rule Elimination [SwT]: optimization of a *decision table* to reduce the number of *rules* it contains.

Rule of Inference [Log]: a rule in a *calculus* which permits *propositions* to be inferred from others given or already inferred.

S

S-**Equivalent** [Log]: of two assertions in *temporal logic*, *equivalent* in a given state *S*.

S-**Valid** [Log]: of an assertion in *temporal logic*, *valid* in a given state *S*.

Safe Net [GNT]: a *k-bounded* net for which $k = 1$.

Safe Rule [Com]: a *computation rule* such that the expansion of a *recursion equation* terminates for all *arguments* in the *domain* of the least *fixpoint* of the equation.

Satisfiable [Log]: of a *predicate formula*, true under at least one *interpretation*.

Scalar (n) [Alg]: an *element* belonging to the *field* associated with a *vector space*.

Scope [Log; Lan; PTh]: of a *variable* in a *formal expression* or program, that part of the expression or program in which all occurrences of the *variable* denote the same object, e.g. scope of a *bound variable* in a *quantifier*; scope of a program *variable*.

Scott Topology the *topology* on a *complete partial order* consisting of all *subsets U* which satisfy both the property that, if x is in U and $x \leq y$, then y is in U, and also the property that, if D is a *directed set* whose *least upper bound* lies in U, then some *element* of D lies in U. Cf. *Alexandroff topology*.

Second Order Predicate Calculus [Log]: a *predicate calculus* in which it is possible to *quantify* over *predicates* as well as *individuals*.

Selection [PTh]: a construct in a programming language permitting one of a collection of mutually alternative actions to be taken, possibly depending on one or more conditions.

Self-Embedding [Lan]: of a *context-free grammar*, possessing a *non-terminal A* such that a *sentential form xAy* can be derived where neither x nor y is the empty *sentence*.

Semantic (adj) [PTh]: see *semantics*.

Semantic Analysis [PPr, PTh]: the analysis of a program to determine whether it obeys the *semantic rules* of the language in which it is written.

Semantic Domain [PTh]: the collection of objects in a *theory* denoted by programs or *specifications* according to the rules of some *denotational semantics*.

Semantic Function [PTh]: a *function* mapping a language construct onto its *denotation*; a *function* in a semantic *metalanguage*.

Semantic Model [PTh]: a *semantic domain* possessing useful formal properties relevant to a particular kind of program or *specification*.

Semantic Rules [PTh]: see *semantics*.

Semantics (n, singular) [PTh]: a system of *rules* according to which the meanings of *sentences* in a *language* are determined.

Semi-Decidability [Com]: that property of a *calculus, canonical system* or *theory* by virtue of which there exists an *algorithm* to decide if one of an identified class of *formulae* possesses a particular property, but which may fail to terminate if the class does not possess that property; see also *decidability*.

Semi-Decidable [Com]: a class of *propositions* is said to be semi-decidable if there exists a *Turing machine* which, given a representation of a *member* of the class, can determine in finite time if the *proposition* is true, but which may fail to terminate if the *proposition* is false; see also *decidable*.

Semi-Formal (adj) [PPr]: see *semi-formal method*.

Semi-Formal Method [PPr]: a method which has some underlying theoretical basis, but which uses both *formal methods* and *heuristic methods* in practice.

Semigroup [Alg]: an *algebraic system* with a single *operation* • which is both *associative* and *closed*.

Semi-Thue Production [Com]: in a *combinatorial system*, a *production* of the form $AxB \rightarrow Ax'B$.

Semi-Thue System [Com]: a *combinatorial system* whose *productions* are all *semi-Thue productions*.

Sentence [Lan]: a *string* of *terminals* derived from the *start symbol* in a *grammar*.

Sentential Form [Lan]: a *string* of *terminals* and *non-terminals* obtained from the *start symbol* at an intermediate stage of a *derivation*.

Separation of Concerns [PPr]: a precept of *structured programming* which holds that programs should be composed so that detailed design of one component can be completed without knowledge of the internal workings of other components.

Sequence [STh]: a *function* whose *domain* is the *set* of *natural numbers* or a contiguous *subset* of them.

Sequential Function [Aut]: a *function computable* by a *sequential machine*.

Sequential Machine [Aut]: generic term including *Mealy automata, Moore automata, complete sequential machines* and *generalised sequential machines*.

Sequential Relation [Aut]: a *relation* such that a *sequential machine* can enumerate the *elements* of the relation.

Service [PPr]: in a *network*, a *set* of processing facilities made available to a *process* by means of a *protocol*.

Set [STh]: a collection of objects.

Set Theory: the branch of mathematics dealing with the properties of *sets* and the *operations* which may be performed upon them.

Simple Ordering (n) [STh]: a *relation* which is *antisymmetric, transitive* and *strongly connected.*

Simultaneous Assignment [PPr, PTh]: multiple *assignment* in which each individual assignment is done in parallel with the others.

Singleton Set [STh]: a *set* with exactly one *element.*

Skolemization [Log]: a procedure for the elimination of *existential quantifiers* from a *predicate formula.*

Soluble [Com]: *decidable* and *computable.*

Sort (n) [PPr, PTh]: the *set* of *denotations* of the values over which a program *variable* may range.

Specification [PPr]: the characterisation of all of the properties of an object relevant to some particular purpose (e.g. program design); the process of producing a specification.

Start Symbol [Lan]: see *grammar.*

State-Transition Diagram [Aut]: a drawn, labelled *graph* representing a *finite state machine* in which *nodes* represent *states* and *arcs* represent *transitions.*

State Space [STh]: the *set* of all possible states of one or a collection of *finite state machines* or other similar systems.

Static Analysis [PPr]: a form of *semantic analysis* which determines compliance with *static semantic rules.*

Static Checking [PPr]: *static analysis.*

Static Semantic Rules [PTh]: see *static semantics.*

Static Semantics [PTh]: the *semantics* of a programming language which may be checked at compile time and is concerned with aspects of the program not related to control flow. Cf. *dynamic semantics.*

Stepwise Refinement [PPr]: a method of *structured design* whereby an *implementation* of a *specification* is devised in terms of high-level components which are resolved in steps into progressively finer levels of detail.

Stop (n) [PTh]: a statement in a *guarded command language* causing all action to cease.

Store (n) [PTh]: of a program, a record of the effect of *assignments.*

Strict Partial Ordering (n) [STh]: a *relation* which is *irreflexive, antisymmetric* and *transitive.*

Strict Simple Ordering (n) [STh]: a *relation* which is *irreflexive, antisymmetric, transitive* and *connected.*

Strictly Decreasing [STh]: of a *sequence* of values from an *ordered set,* such that each value is exceeded by its predecessor.

Strictly Increasing [STh]: of a *sequence* of values from an *ordered set,* such that each value exceeds its predecessor.

String [Gen]: a *finite sequence* of symbols.

Strong Eventual Fairness [PTh]: a property of a system with respect to an *inductive assertion* such that the system cannot pass through infinitely many states in which the assertion may eventually become true without its actually becoming true. Cf. *weak eventual fairness.*

Strongly Connected [GNT]: of a *directed graph,* such that there is a *path* from each *vertex* to every other *vertex*; [STh]: a *relation R* is strongly connected with respect to a *set A* if for all x and y in A it contains at least one of the *ordered pairs* $<x, y>$ and $<y, x>$.

Strong Typing [PPr, PTh]: a strict kind of *typing* in which only a *variable* of a given type may be used in contexts where that type is explicitly cited.

Structural Correspondence [PPr]: in *JSP*, the condition that there is a *computable homomorphism* from the inputs to the outputs of a program.

Structural Induction [Com]: a form of *Noetherian induction* in which properties of a *recursion scheme* are proved with respect to the *syntactic* structure of the scheme.

Structure [Gen]: a property of a system whereby complex characteristics depend on combinations of simpler ones.

Structure Clash [PPr]: in *JSP*, an absence of *structural correspondence*.

Structure Diagram [PPr]: in *JSP*, a diagram representing the *control structure* of a program.

Structured Design [PPr]: *design* imparting *structure*.

Structured Programming [PPr]: programming using *structured design*, *structured testing* and any methods supporting them.

Structured Testing [PPr]: testing of the components of systems in an order corresponding to the structure of the system.

Subgraph [GNT]: a *graph* $G_1 = (V_1, A_1)$ is a *subgraph* of graph $G_2 = (V_2, A_2)$ if and only if V_1 is a *subset* of V_2 and A_1 is a *subset* of A_2. Cf. *partial graph*.

Subset [STh]: of a *set A*, a *set B* such that *A includes B*.

Successor [Gen]: see *successor function*.

Successor Function [Gen]: a *function* from the *natural numbers* to the *natural numbers* such that no two distinct numbers have the same successor, no number has *zero* as its successor, and every natural number may be obtained from *zero* by a *finite* number of applications of the successor function.

Sufficient Condition [Log]: P is a sufficient condition for Q if and only if $P \Rightarrow Q$.

Summation [PTh]: in *CCS*, *polyadic parallel composition*.

Surjective [STh]: of a *function*, such that the *range* (in general a *subset* of the *codomain*) is equal to the *codomain*.

Symbol Table [PPr]: a table of properties of *lexemes* used by a translator during *syntax analysis*.

Symmetric [STh]: of a *relation R*, having the property that whenever $<x, y>$ is in R then so is $<y, x>$.

Symmetric Difference [STh]: of two *sets A* and *B*, the *union* of the *difference A - B* and the *difference B - A*.

Synchronisation Tree [PTh]: in *CCS*, a *tree* representing possible sequences of *synchronised* communication between *processes*.

Synchronised [PTh]: of two *events*, occurring at the same time.

Syntactic [Gen]: see *syntax*.

Syntactic Domain [PTh]: a *set* of language constructs mapped onto a *semantic domain* by a *semantic function*.

Syntax [PTh]: *grammar* (used in connection with programming theory).

Syntax Analysis [PPr]: *parsing* of program text, usually taking place in an early pass of a compiler.

T

Tape (n): a conceptual part of an *automaton* upon which input *strings*, intermediate working results and output *strings* may be written.

Target [STh]: *range*.

Tautology [Log]: a *proposition* which is true under all possible *interpretations*, e.g. $P \Rightarrow P$.

Temporal Logic [Log]: the branch of *logic* dealing with reasoning from statements involving auxiliary verbs of tense.

Temporal Ordering [Gen]: *ordering* in time.

Terminal (n) [Lan]: see *grammar*.

Ternary [Gen]: pertaining to three, e.g. ternary *relation*. Cf. *unary*, *binary*, *n-ary*.

Theorem [Gen]: an unconditionally *derived* result in a *calculus* or *theory*.

Theorem Prover [SwT, PTh]: a software tool used to find *derivations* of *theorems*, especially in connection with *program verification*.

Theory [Gen]: a *calculus* in which the *axioms* assert the existence of *primitive* objects.

Timeout [PPr]: in a system of co-operating *processes*, failure of a process to achieve something within a specified period.

Token [GNT]: an object occupying a *place* in a *Petri net*.

Token Colouring [GNT]: an abstract means of distinguishing groups of *tokens* to be treated separately in a *Petri net*, by assigning distinct notional colours to each group.

Top-Down Design [PPr]: *stepwise refinement*.

Top-Down Development [PPr]: program development using *top-down design*.

Top-Down Parsing [Lan]: a *parsing* method associated with *LL(K) grammars* in which a procedure generating a *leftmost derivation* is driven by the text to be parsed.

Topological Space [Top]: a *set A* and a *topology* on A.

Topology [Top]: on a set A, a collection ϑ of *subsets* of A, called *open sets*, such that

1. A and the *empty set* φ are both in ϑ;
2. if B and C are in ϑ, then the *intersection* $B \cap C$ is in ϑ;
3. if ϑ' is any *subset* of ϑ, then the *union* of all the *elements* of ϑ' is in ϑ.

Total Function [STh]: see *function*.

Totally Correct [PTh]: of a program, *partially correct* and always progressing to termination.

Total Ordering [STh]: a *connected partial ordering*.

Total Recursive Function [Com]: a *general recursive function* defined for all values of its arguments. Cf. *partial recursive function*.

Transition [Aut]: an actual or possible change of state of an *automaton*; [GNT]: a *vertex* in a *Petri net* which, in *firing* conveys *tokens* from its *input places* to its *output places*.

Transition Function [Aut]: of a *Mealy automaton*, a *partial function* from $S \times I$ into $S \times O$.

Transitive [STh]: of a *relation R*, having the property that whenever $<x, y>$ and $<y, z>$ are both in R then $<x, z>$ is in R.

Traversal [PPr]: enumeration of the items in a *data structure*, especially a *tree*.

Tree [GNT]: an *undirected, connected* and *acyclic graph*; a *directed graph* with a designated *vertex v* (the *root* of the tree) such that there are no *arcs* of the form (u,v), and for every *arc* of the form (v,u), u is the *root* of a directed tree; [PPr]: a linked *data structure* connected in the manner of a tree.

Truth Valuation [Log]: evaluation of a logical *formula* by assigning an *interpretation* to its parts.

Tuple [STh]: a *sequence* of one or more values. See also *n-tuple*.

Turing Machine [Com]: the most powerful of *abstract* machines definable as a 5-*tuple* (S, A, T, s_1, F) where S is a *non-empty set* of *states*, A is the machine's *alphabet*, T is a *mapping* from $S \times A$ into $S \times A$ specifying *operations* on a conceptual *tape*, s_1 is the initial state and F is a *set* of final states.

Type 0 Grammar [Lan]: a *grammar*.

Type 0 Language [Lan]: a *language generated* by a *type 0 grammar*.

Type 1 Grammar [Lan]: a *grammar* in which for every *production* $X \to Y$, both X and Y are *strings* of *non-terminals* and *terminals* and the length of Y is no less than that of X.

Type 1 Language [Lan]: a *language generated* by a *type 1 grammar*.

Type 2 Grammar [Lan]: a *grammar* whose *productions* are all of the form $A \to X$ where A is a *non-terminal* and X is a *string* of *non-terminals* and *terminals*.

Type 2 Language [Lan]: a *language generated* by a *type 2 grammar*.

Type 3 Grammar [Lan]: a *grammar* whose *productions* are all of the form $A \to aB$ or $A \to a$, where A and B are *non-terminals* and a is a *terminal*.

Type 3 Language [Lan]: a *language generated* by a *type 3 grammar*.

Typing [PPr, PTh]: the restriction of *values* of a *variable* denoted by an *identifier* in a programming language to a particular *domain* in the underlying *calculus* or *theory*.

U

Unary [Gen]: pertaining to one, e.g. unary *operation*. Cf. *binary, ternary, n-ary*.

Uncountable [STh]: of an *infinite set*, not *countable*.

Undirected Graph [GNT]: see *graph*.

Unification [Log]: the *algorithm* underlying *resolution methods*.

Union [STh]: of two *sets A* and *B*, the *set* whose *elements* are exactly those in either A or B (or both); the union of A and B is commonly denoted by

$A \cup B$. More generally, the union of any *set* ϑ of *sets* consists of those *elements* lying in at least one of the *sets* in ϑ; see *polyadic union*.

Unit Set [STh]: *singleton set*.

Universal Quantifier [Log]: a *quantifier* usually written '$\forall x$' and read 'for all x'. Cf. *existential quantifier*.

Universal Set [STh]: the *set* to which all objects under consideration belong.

Unobservable [Aut, PTh]: not detectable from outward behaviour.

Unordered Pair [STh]: a *set* of the form $\{x, y\}$.

Until [Log]: a derived operator in *temporal logic* such that the assertion A until B expresses the condition that A will remain true until B becomes true.

Upper Bound [STh]: of a *subset* T of a *set* S with a *partial ordering* $\leq$, an *element* x of S such that $y \leq x$ for all y in S.

V

Vacuous [Log]: of a *quantifier*, having no occurrences of its *bound variable* in its *scope*.

Valid [Log]: of a predicate *formula*, true under all possible *interpretations*.

Validation [Gen]: the testing of a system to determine whether it complies with given requirements, particularly the requirements of a standard.

Value [STh]: an *element* of the *range* of a *function*.

Variable [Gen]: an object denoted by an *identifier* in a *calculus* or programming language; [Lan] a *non-terminal*.

Vector Space [Alg]: an *algebraic system* comprising a *set V* of *elements* called 'vectors' with an *operation* '+' and a *field* of *scalars F* such that V is an *Abelian group* with respect to +, and such that any vector A in V and any scalar c in F determine a 'scalar product' $c \cdot A \in V$ with the properties

1. $c \cdot (A + B) = c \cdot A + c \cdot B$;
2. $c \cdot (d \cdot A) = cd \cdot A$; and
3. $e \cdot A = A$ where e is the *identity element* of F under $\cdot$.

Verification [PTh]: proof of a property of an object which is the subject of a *formal model* by means of reasoning in the *calculus* or *theory* in terms of which the meaning of the model is defined.

Vertex [GNT]: an element of a *graph*. Two vertices may be connected to each another by an *arc*.

Vienna Definition Language [PTh]: a semantic *metalanguage* used to define the programming language PL/1, forming the basis of the later *VDM-SL*.

Vienna Development Method (VDM) [PTh]: a *formal development method* with three components: a notation for expressing software specification, design and development; an inference system for constructing formal proofs of correctness; and a methodological framework for developing software from a specification in a formally verifiable manner.

VDM Specification Language (VDM-SL) [PTh]: the *metalanguage* of *VDM*.

W

Weakest Pre-Condition [PTh]: in a *guarded command language*, the least specific *pre-condition* such that a command terminates.

Weak Eventual Fairness [PTh]: a property of a system with respect to an *inductive assertion* such that the system will not proceed indefinitely without the assertion becoming true. Cf. *strong eventual fairness*.

Weakly Connected [GNT]: of a *directed graph*, such that the corresponding *undirected graph* formed by replacing each *ordered pair* of *vertices* by an *unordered pair* is connected.

Weak Typing [PPr, PTh]: *typing* which is not *strong typing*.

Weight [GNT]: a value associated with an *arc* of a *graph*.

Well-Formed [Gen.]: complying with given *formation rules*.

Well-Ordering (n) [STh]: a *total ordering* on a *set S* in which every *non-empty subset* of *S* has a *least element*.

Well-Ordering Principle [STh]: the *axiom* that, for any *set S*, there is a *well ordering* on *S*; equivalent to the *Axiom of Choice* and to *Zorn's Lemma*.

Word [Lan]: a *string* whose symbols lie in some specified *finite set*.

Z

Zero [Gen]: the *natural number* which is not the *successor* of any other natural number.

Zero Element [Alg]: in a *ring*, the *identity element* for the additive *operation*.

Zorn's Lemma [STh]: the *axiom* that, if *S* is a *set* with a *partial ordering* ≤, and if every *non-empty subset* of *S* on which ≤ is a *total ordering* has an *upper bound*, then *S* has a *maximal element*; equivalent to the *Axiom of Choice* and the *Well-Ordering Principle*.